EDMONDSON TICKETS
OF THE
NORTH LONDON RAILWAY
AND
ASSOCIATED RAILWAYS

DAVID G GELDARD

The Transport Ticket Society
2001

Comments etc. regarding this publication are welcome;
please write to the Society's Publications Officer:

David Harman
24 Frankfield Rise
Tunbridge Wells
TN2 5LF

E-Mail: David.Harman@btinternet.com

ISBN 0 903209 49 7

Published by
The Transport Ticket Society
1 Winchester Drive, Muxton,Telford, TF2 8SJ

Printed by
Paterson Printing Ltd,
Tunbridge Wells

Introduction,
Sources and Acknowledgements

On many occasions I have picked up my North London tickets and vowed that I will really try and make sense of an extremely complex subject. I have then decided that I could not do it justice in view of the difficulties caused both by gaps in essential information and by the wide range of different ticket markings and through booking facilities. This time, however, despite lacking understanding of some features of practice, particularly in the early years, I decided that some published record should be produced. I am aware of its deficiencies, if anybody is able to correct me on any point, or to add any further information I will be most grateful.

The work deals with the North London Rly itself, with its forerunner the East & West India Docks & Birmingham Junction Rly, with the Hampstead Junction Rly down to the time when its ticket supplies were taken over by the London & North Western Rly and with the North & South Western Junction Railway. When dealing with the opening and closing of lines and stations "on and from" dates for public passenger services are used.

The familiar pasteboard railway ticket, measuring 2¼ by 1³/₁₆ inches, was the invention of Thomas Edmondson. Having commenced railway employment with the Newcastle & Carlisle Rly in 1836 he moved to the Manchester & Leeds Rly in May 1839, leaving them in 1841 to establish his own business producing tickets and associated machinery. The company went under the title of John B Edmondson Limited, John being Thomas's son. This work uses the now accepted convention of showing Edmondson if the ticket was a product of the company of that name, and edmondson as a generic term for all pasteboard tickets of the given size.

The backs of all tickets described are blank (unprinted), unless stated otherwise. An appendix shows printed backs that were in use, and reference codes from the appendix are used as necessary throughout this work.

Primary sources consulted at the Public Record Office are as follows:

Minutes of Board Meetings 1850-1922	RAIL 529/11-34
Minutes of Officers Meetings 1862-85	RAIL 529/38-40
Minutes of Stores & Report Committees 1862-71	RAIL 529/41
Minutes of Locomotive & Stores Committee 1865-71	RAIL 529/42-44
Minutes of Locomotive Stores & Traffic Committee 1871-1909	RAIL 529/45-64
Minutes of Officers Meetings 1909-19	RAIL 529/83-85
General Orders 1862-1907	RAIL 529/110
Historical File 1864-1903	RAIL 529/113
Various NLR public timetables	

Secondary sources include much of the work of the late H.V. Borley, an eminent authority on London's railways, in particular:

- an article entitled The North London Railway in the *Railway & Canal Historical Society Journal* Volume VIII, page 39, dated May 1962.
- an article in *The Railway Magazine* dated February 1964,
- *Chronology of London Railways*, published 1982 by the RCHS,
- unpublished manuscripts in the library of The Railway Club.

Other secondary sources include Jim Connor's *Broad Street to Poplar* and *Broad Street to Primrose Hill*, Michael Robbin's Oakwood History of the line, articles in *Railway Magazine* and other periodicals and the standard histories of those companies with whom the NLR had through running or booking arrangements.

In addition to my own ticket collection I have also studied those of John Butcher, Jim Connor, Godfrey Croughton, Martin Rickitt, John Shelbourn and Michael Stewart and of the late Frank Casserley, Trefor David and Charles Gordon Stuart, together with the tickets held by the National Railway Museum and the Public Record Office. I am grateful to all for their assistance.

I owe a real debt to Jim Connor, who was kind enough to read my final manuscript and to correct me on a number of points. I take full responsibility for any remaining errors.

Finally, my thanks to David Harman for preparing the maps and for formatting and presenting this work in a form fit for publication.

David Geldard
Stratford-upon-Avon
October 2001

Contents

༺༻

Chapter One

1850-1852; THE EAST & WEST INDIA DOCKS AND BIRMINGHAM JUNCTION RAILWAY

The E&WID&BJR originated from a wish of the London & Birmingham Railway to reach the docks on the River Thames. The latter company amalgamated with the Grand Junction Railway and the Manchester & Birmingham Railway on 16 July 1846 to form the London & North Western Railway. The L&NWR supplied the majority of capital for the E&WID&BJR, the intention being that the line would be worked by the L&NWR for goods traffic only. From the opening, however, carriage of passengers was to take pride of place.

The first section of the line opened on 26 September 1850, from Islington to Bow and thence to a junction with the London & Blackwall Railway. A quarter-hourly train service was provided from the Fenchurch Street terminus of the L&BR calling at Stepney (L&B), Bow, Hackney and Islington. Trains to Fenchurch Street were up, those from Fenchurch Street were down.

On opening, only single journey tickets were issued and a flat fare system was in operation between any two NLR stations at fares of 6d first class and 4d second class. Flat fares were not used for bookings to and from L&BR stations, the revenue from these was split according to the distance travelled on each company's line. It seems probable that through bookings to L&BR stations east of Stepney (Limehouse, West India Docks, Poplar and Blackwall) were also available from the earliest days.

Figure 1 shows a card sent to H.V. Borley in 1935 giving a sketch of, and notes on, an opening day ticket; the original has not been traced. It is described as printed on pale blue paper, the reverse being buff-brown paper. In his *RCHS Journal* paper, Borley states that this is a single ticket and, even though it is clearly a half edmondson, he is likely to be correct. A Board Minute of 18 July 1850 states that *"The Directors also recommend the adoption of Edmondson's ticket system with some slight modifications which have been suggested with a view towards the reduction of expense"*. The L&BR are known to have been using Edmondsons by late August 1841. Not until 29 November 1850 do the Minutes record that *"The issue of double tickets with a view to encouraging passenger traffic was discussed and it was resolved that they should be issued at fares of 9d. 1st class and 6d. 2nd class from such stations as may be deemed expedient."* This leads to the clear presumption that the ticket shown in Figure 1 is indeed a single, and that possibly the reduction of expense resulted from the use of half size edmondsons or even (although much more unlikely) of the earliest "double singles", i.e. two singles printed on one standard sized card to be bisected before issue. It is not known for how long the small tickets remained in use, Borley states that *"a few years after opening of the railway tickets of normal size were adopted for local journeys"*. However, no authority is given and other evidence suggests the use of standard size edmondsons as early as 1853.

A station at Kingsland was opened on 9 November 1850 and the line was extended beyond Islington to Camden Town on 7 December 1850. Three days before that, the Board decision of 29 November was implemented and return tickets were introduced. No particular stations are recorded in the Minutes, presumably returns were issued at all stations.

On 19 December it was reported to the Board that as the second class fares were generally below the Parliamentary rate of 1d per mile the Commissioners of Railways had approved all the company's trains as Parliamentary Trains when the actual fare paid did not exceed 1d per mile. However, one train a day each way had to be run for intermediate distances where special fares were necessary to bring them below the necessary rate. Thus, in addition to the flat fare tickets Parliamentary singles were also in use; these would have been required for journeys not exceeding 3 miles, i.e. at a fare of 3d or less. As the company did not provide third class accommodation Parliamentary passengers travelled in the second class coaches.

The Parliamentary fare was a consequence of the Railway Regulation Act of 1844, in force from 1 November that year.

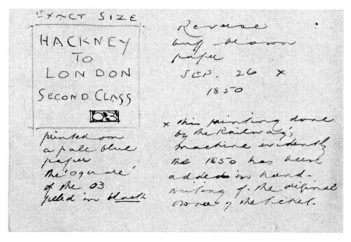

Figure 1

3

Section 6 required that all passenger railway companies, every weekday, except Christmas Day and Good Friday, and on Sundays too, if Sunday trains were run, should run at least one train along their lines from end to end, including branches, in each direction, starting at an hour fixed by the directors subject to the approval of the Lords of the Committee of the Privy Council for Trade and Plantations. The speed was not to be less than 12 miles an hour, including stoppages at every station, and the carriages were to be provided with seats protected from the weather. The fare was not to exceed one penny per mile, with children under three years age free and of three but under twelve years at half fare. In return the railway company was relieved from the 5% passenger duty on receipts from the Parliamentary tickets issued for these trains.

Return fares proved to be a cause of some contention with the L&BR. On 23 May 1851 the E&WID&BJR Board recorded objection by the L&BR to their issue and the lowered revenue that resulted from the offered reduction of one quarter on twice the single fare. It was noted that the NLR reduction in fact exactly matched the reduction given by the L&BR on their own local return fares!

The line was further extended to a temporary station at Hampstead Road on 9 June 1851 and a new station at Caledonian Road was opened on 10 June 1852. On the same date the Minutes recorded that season tickets are to be issued from 1 July 1852, first class only at a charge of 10 guineas per annum. Season tickets are a subject in themselves, and do not fall within the scope of this work.

ઠ૪ભ

Chapter Two

1853-1859; THE NORTH LONDON RAILWAY and NORTH & SOUTH WESTERN JUNCTION RAILWAY

On 1 January 1853 the E&WID&BJR changed its name to the North London Railway.

On 7 April 1853 the Board heard that a compromise over return fares had been reached with the L&BR, such fares from the NLR to stations east of Stepney being increased to twice the single fare on Sundays only. On 1 April 1855 all NLR returns were increased to twice the single fare, i.e. to 1/- and 8d respectively, but traffic fell so much that day returns were made available from 1 June at 10d and 7d. Even this did not retrieve the situation and the original return fares of 9d and 6d were restored on 3 September 1855.

The principal event of 1853 was the opening of the N&SWJR from Willesden Junction, with the L&NWR, to Kew Old Junction with the Windsor Loop of the London & South Western Rly. This took place for passenger traffic on 1 August 1853, stations being provided at Acton and Kew. The January 1856 timetable shows fares between the two N&SWJR stations as single 6d first class, 4d second class and return 9d and 6d respectively.

Accounts of early working to the N&SWJR vary, there is some suggestion of through carriages but Borley thought that except for one express working for a few months from 21 October 1857 all Kew passengers had to change at Hampstead Road. Either way, haulage from Hampstead Road was by L&NWR locomotives and L&NWR metals were used between Hampstead Road and the N&SWJR. The Board were advised that the total mileage from Fenchurch Street to Kew was 18 miles, made up of L&BR 2½, NLR 7½, L&NWR 4 and N&SWJR 4. Through first class fares were 1/3d single, 1/9d return, with second class being 1/- single and 1/4d return. The

NLR looked upon the N&SWJR as an extension of its own line, and always treated N&SWJR stations as local for ticket purposes.

Camden Town station was renamed Camden Road in 1853, the exact date does not appear to be known. The white ordinary single shown in Figure 2 was probably printed shortly thereafter. The back is plain white.

Figure 2

In the Board Minutes for 7 July 1853 it is recorded that Messrs. Smith Bros., who have advertised on the Company's stations and in their second class carriages, have offered to meet the entire cost of printing the Company's tickets for the privilege of printing approved advertisements on the back. The tickets then cost the Company approximately £370 per year to print, and no objection was seen to accepting the offer with proper regulations.

Figure 3 shows an ordinary return on yellow card with a black transverse stripe and with a plain yellow back. The likelihood is that it is from the original stock supplied for the opening of the N&SWJR on 1 August 1853. The white return ticket of Figure 4 carries on a green back the advertisement shown in Figure 5, presumably it took some time to implement the

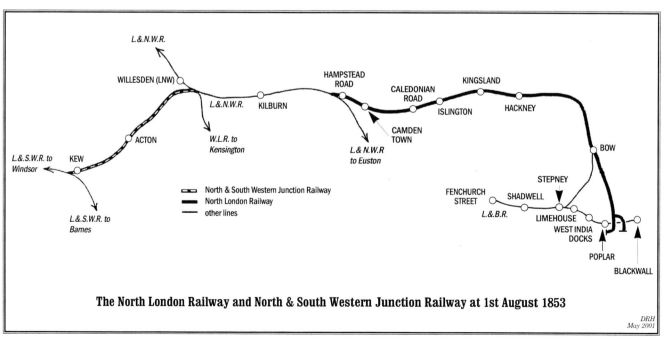

The North London Railway and North & South Western Junction Railway at 1st August 1853

DRH
May 2001

Figure 3

Figure 4

Figure 5

advertisement system and the assumption is thus that the Figure 4 ticket is later than that of Figure 3.

Figures 6 to 8 show what were possibly the next developments of ordinary returns, the yellow ticket of Figure 6 carries

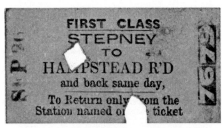

Figure 6

Figure 7

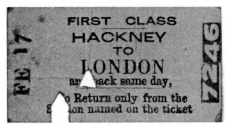

Figure 8

availability notices and has the advertisement of Figure 7 on a buff back while the front of the white ticket of Figure 8 has the same format as that of Figure 6 but the back is plain white and unprinted. This could indicate quite a short life for the use of advertisements; after 7 July 1853 there is no further reference to these in any of the primary source Minutes.

On 21 November 1855 the Board considered the system of ticket collecting, the Minute states that it appears to expose the company to fraud both by passengers and staff. The only recommendation was "*a certain cut of the facility afforded to passengers for leaving the station quickly after their journey by collection of tickets after travel*". A communication was sent to the L&BR urging them to adopt the more usual method of collection; that company agreed and collection of tickets at the end of the journey commenced on 1 January 1856.

The clear conclusion to be drawn from this is that until 1856 tickets were collected on or before entering the trains. This would not have caused the L&BR any problems as they also operated a flat fare system, and indeed there would have been no difficulty for the NLR over their own flat fare bookings. There were, however, potential problems with station to station Parliamentary tickets and also with station to station tickets between the L&BR, the NLR and the N&SWJR. Collecting these before the journey commenced clearly exposed the company to unchecked over-travelling, and it must have been this abuse that the Board were addressing.

Collection before travel is straightforward for single journey tickets, but what of returns? Figures 3, 4, 6 and 8 show the only local returns known that are likely to be pre-1856 and, logically, they are in single coupon format. Thus, the ticket would simply have been inspected (and probably clipped) prior to the outward journey and left in the passenger's possession for collection prior to the return journey. It is worth observing that contemporary L&BR returns were also single coupon.

Following the logic of the preceding paragraph, two-coupon returns such as those of Figures 9 to 11 are likely to be of types introduced after 1 January 1856. Figure 9 shows the yellow return half of a ticket from the L&BR to the N&SWJR, the showing of Fenchurch Street rather than simply London is noteworthy. Presumably this was because of the possibility of returning to Euston via the L&NWR, an option not open to passengers to and from NLR stations. Figures 10 and 11 show return halves of flat fare tickets, the former (white) issued outward to any NLR station and the latter (red) issued outward to any L&BR station. A return half similar to that of Figure 11 but showing "No. 1" is also known. Possibly the

Figure 9

Figure 10

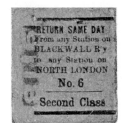

Figure 11

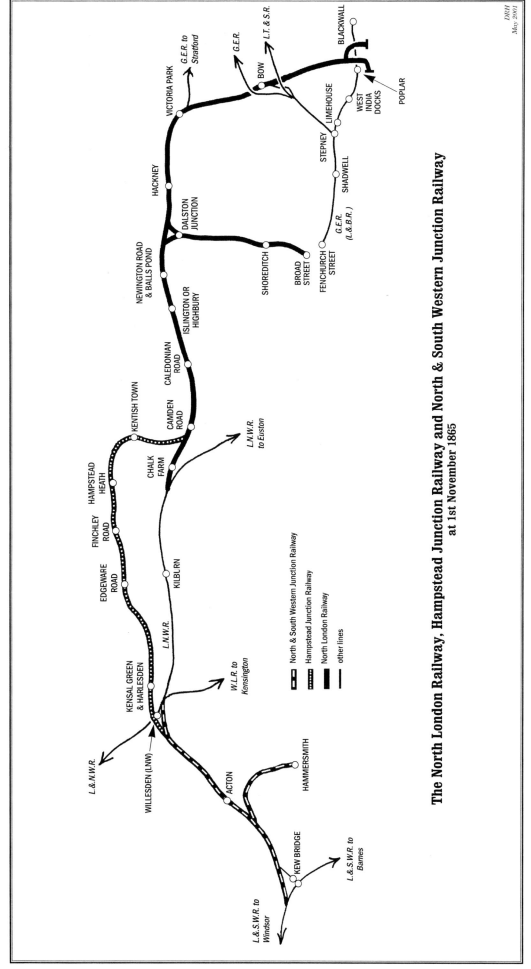

The North London Railway, Hampstead Junction Railway and North & South Western Junction Railway
at 1st November 1865

thick black lines top and bottom distinguished the tickets as issued to the L&BR.

Borley's records include sketches of a flat fare single and return, re-created as Figures 12 and 13. Clearly the return half of Figure 13 reproduces the type shown in Figure 10.

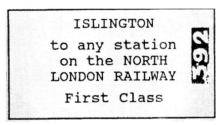

Figure 12

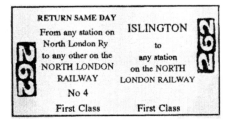

Figure 13

Borley states that the first class tickets were white, the second class red and that No 4 was at that time the number of Islington station. If it is assumed that station numbering commenced at Hampstead Road (as it did in the later 1865 system) then prior to the opening of Victoria Park to regular passenger traffic on 14 June 1856, the numbers would have been:

1	Hampstead Road
2	Camden Road
3	Caledonian Road
4	Islington
5	Kingsland (Figure 10)
6	Hackney (Figure 11)
7	Bow

Note, however, that as Islington was the middle one of seven stations the reverse order is also possible! Opening of Victoria Park (between Hackney and Bow), would affect the numbering, as would the opening of Newington Road (between Islington and Kingsland) on 1 September 1858.

Colours of known flat fare tickets are consistent with those given by Borley. It is likely that directional colouring was used for station to station tickets for most of the period from 1850 to 1865, known tickets suggesting that (ignoring any stripes) first class up singles, up halves of two-coupon returns and single coupon returns with an up return journey, i.e. towards Fenchurch Street, were yellow and corresponding

down tickets were white. If later practice was followed then corresponding second class colours would have been blue and red respectively. No suggestion is made as to the colours of Parliamentary tickets. The stripe on the ticket of Figure 3 may have signified a journey beyond the limits of the NLR. The use of one stripe only indicated a first class ticket.

A permanent station was opened at Hampstead Road to the west of the temporary one on 5 May 1855. A branch of the N&SWJR to Hammersmith opened to passengers on 8 April 1858, for much of the time during the next few years the Kew train dropped a composite brake carriage at Acton Gatehouse Junction, which was then worked to Hammersmith. On the up journey the Kew train stopped for the Hammersmith carriage to be attached.

1860-1865; THE HAMPSTEAD JUNCTION RAILWAY

In order to avoid congestion north of Camden the L&NWR promoted the nominally independent Hampstead Junction Railway, from a junction with the NLR near Camden Road to a junction with the N&SWJR at Old Oak, together with a spur to the L&NWR at Harlesden. This was opened on 2 January 1860 with stations at Kentish Town, Hampstead Heath, Finchley Road and Edgeware Road.

A service then started between Camden Road and Edgeware Road, with some trains running through to Kew and a few going beyond over the L&SWR to Twickenham or Kingston. Passengers between NLR Main Line stations and HJR or N&SWJR stations were required to change at Camden Road, although from 1 February 1860 some through carriages were attached/detached at Camden Road. Through running of NLR trains via Kilburn appears to have ceased. From 1 January 1865 the HJR was, by agreement with the L&NWR, treated as an integral part of the NLR. Unfortunately, nothing is known of tickets on the HJR prior to this date, although there is no reason to think that NLR practice was not followed, as was clearly the case later.

A new station at Kensal Green & Harlesden was opened on 1 November 1861, Hampstead Road was renamed Chalk Farm on 1 December 1862 and Islington was renamed Islington or Highbury on 1 June 1864. Platforms for NLR trains were opened at the L&SWR Kew Bridge station on 1 February 1862 and this then became the principal station for trains over the N&SWJR, Kew closing for regular passenger traffic.

On 15 December 1863 it was reported to the Board that the numbers of tickets issued between adjacent stations were low, and it was resolved that from 1 January 1864 the fares for these be halved (to 3d and 2d single) and the result reported in six months. The new Short Journey fares were successful, special tickets were designed and, as will be seen, they remained a feature of NLR practice for a number of years.

෨൫ඣ

Chapter Three

TICKET SUPPLIERS 1850 - 1912

It will be remembered that prior to opening of the E&WID&BJR the Board resolved to use Edmondson's ticket system, this in itself does not mean that Edmondson were the ticket suppliers but it is clear that the NLR did not attempt to print their own tickets and there must be a strong presumption that tickets were bought from Edmondson, which also supplied the L&BR. The tickets of Figures 2 to 13, all thought to be from the 1850s, all give the impression of being typical Edmondson products. Characteristic features are the use of negatively printed serial numbers facing outwardly of the ticket, the numbers being impressed from two separate wheels, one printing tens and units and the other thousands and hundreds.

Only two tickets are known which are definitely or probably from the early 1860s. That of Figure 14, on blue card, is likely to be from Edmondson, it is not an ordinary local issue but is included here as it gives valuable dating information. The front is enigmatic, happily the ticket was retained by Frederic Yeats Edwards, a Victorian railway enthusiast who kept a diary on the back of tickets issued to him. His note on the back of this ticket reads "Wimbledon Review. 12 July 1862." Presumably it was for a special train to Wimbledon (via the then quite new Kew Bridge curve) for that event, but there is no indication as to the NLR station at which Edwards joined that train.

Figure 14

Figure 15

The yellow ticket of Figure 15 is more straightforward, the journey would have been made via Stepney and the L&BR. It is important to note the different printing style, in particular the use of positive numerals for the serial number.

On 4 May 1865 the Locomotive & Stores Committee considered tenders for tickets, ticket cases and dating presses from Edmondson and from Messrs. Waterlow and resolved that Waterlow's tender be accepted and a three year contract

entered into commencing on 1 July. On 30 June 1868 Waterlow's tender for a further three years at a cost of 1/3d per thousand tickets was accepted. In 1871 tenders were requested from Edmondson, Waterlow and Messrs. de la Rue & Co. Again, Waterlow were successful at 1/3d per thousand tickets, a 7½% discount off published prices of ticket cases and dating presses at £2-2-0 each. This last tender list is particularly interesting, no other indication is known that de la Rue were involved in printing edmondsons.

The relationship with Waterlow was then to last until 1912, from 1 July 1875 prices were 1/3d per thousand single tickets and 1/4d per thousand returns, from 1 July 1878 dating presses and ticket cases were removed from the contract, tickets themselves continuing to be supplied at the same prices. Renewal was effected from 1 July 1881 and 1884, Waterlow undertaking to deliver the tickets to the stations within eight days of requisition.

The Locomotive Stores & Traffic Committee Minutes then show contract renewal every three years up to and including 1896, prices for ordinary singles and returns staying the same but discounts varying. In 1887 the discount was 5%, which the Committee estimated would save £70 per annum. A little arithmetic then gives supply of approximately 22 million tickets per annum. This is confirmed by returns of uncollected tickets, given every month in the LS&TC Minutes; a typical figure is that for October 1887 recording issue of 1,848,065 tickets with 36,042 (1.95%) missing. Issue per month remained consistent around the 1.7 to 1.8 million figure until towards the end of the century when it had dropped to about 1.6 million, falling further to about 1.4 million in 1902/3.

After 1896 responsibility for renewal of the Waterlow contract fell to the main Board; they approved a new three year contract from 1 July 1899 at prices per thousand for singles 1/3d, returns 1/4d, special machine workman's tickets 1/6d or extra thick 2/3d, excursion 2/- and childrens' tickets with pieces cut out 1/- per thousand extra. Discounts from 2½% to 5% were allowed. In 1902 a five year contract was approved at the same prices except that returns were reduced to 1/3d per thousand.

In 1907 the Board also asked the Bell Punch & Printing Company Limited to tender, approximate costs per annum were recorded as £807 for Waterlow and £969 for Bell Punch. Not surprisingly the contract was again awarded to Waterlow.

On 16 May 1912 the Board noted that the Waterlow contract terminated on 30 June, and recorded that from that date it was proposed to print all tickets in the L&NWR ticket printing department at actual cost to the NLR, which will be slightly under the charges from Waterlow, who had intimated that an increase would be necessary. The long relationship with Waterlow thus came to an end, it was reported in December that the saving on the last half year had been £26.

The Wimbledon Review ticket of Figure 14 shows that Edmondson were the likely printers for the NLR in mid-1862, Waterlow are proven as printers from mid-1865, but what of the three intervening years? From 1865 onwards tenders were requested at three-yearly intervals, this could have been a continuation of earlier practice (nothing is recorded in the Minutes) so suggesting a round of tenders in 1862. The ticket of Figure 15 is definitely not an Edmondson product, nor does it resemble the later Waterlow prints. Clearly there is a possibility that a third party (perhaps de la Rue?) won an 1862 tender, an alternative but unlikely suggestion is that Edmondson found it impossible to meet a particular order in time and some emergency printing was done by a third party.

To finish this chapter on a human note, the Salaries Committee on 19 October 1865 resolved that ticket clerks and sorters should be transferred from the Traffic Department to a new Ticket Section within the Audit Office. That Section was to comprise one ticket checking clerk, one ticket supply clerk, two assistants, one lad and a messenger. The accountancy and audit staff were then located at Camden, plans were approved for a new office building for them at Broad Street in June 1870.

&CG

Chapter Four

THE CITY EXTENSION

On 1 November 1865 the NLR opened its City Extension line with a new terminus at Broad Street and intermediate stations at Shoreditch and Dalston Junction. On the same day Kingsland station was closed, the through east - west connection thereafter only being used for through trains to other companies' lines.

The running direction from the Western and Eastern Junctions at Dalston towards Broad Street was up, all trains left Broad Street in the down direction. Importantly, the running directions of the existing lines were not changed.

In anticipation of the opening Robert Mansel, the General Manager, issued General Order No. 32 dated September 1865, dealing with ticket arrangements and cancelling General Order No. 2 dated 30 January 1863. The latter is unfortunately pasted into the PRO's guard book, the visible side deals exclusively with season tickets, the other may have covered ordinary tickets. It is worth quoting extensively from the ordinary tickets section of G.O.32.

"1. Ordinary Tickets issued for "Up" and "Down" Trains respectively are distinguished by colour as under:-

	UP TRAINS	DOWN TRAINS
First Class	Yellow	White
Second Class	Blue	Red
Third Class	Green with two *transverse* black stripes	Buff with two *transverse* black stripes

2. Tickets between Stations on the City Extension Line and Stations east of Dalston Junction, being available by Trains which pass in either direction over both the Up and Down Lines, are of the ordinary colours but distinguished by a narrow *transverse* stripe of the colour for the Line opposite to that denoted by the colour of the Ticket.

These Tickets are not available for Stations west of Dalston Junction, nor are Tickets issued for Stations west of Dalston available for Stations east of the Junction.

5. Short Journey Tickets available only at the Stations next to that from which they are issued, are of the ordinary colours, but distinguished by a broad stripe (First Class red, Second Class white) carried across the Ticket *longitudinally*, they have also printed on the face the distinctive number or letter of the issuing station, as under:

North London Railway		Hampstead Junc Rly	
Chalk Farm	1	Camden Road	A
Camden Road	2	Kentish Town	B
Caledonian Road	3	Hampstead Heath	C
Highbury	4	Finchley Road	D
Newington Road	5	Edgeware Road	E
Kingsland	6	Kensal Green	F
Hackney	7		
Victoria Park	8	**N&SW Junc Rly**	
Bow	9		
Poplar	P	Acton	G
Dalston Junction	N	Hammersmith	H
Shoreditch	S	Kew	K
Broad Street	L		

COLLECTION OF TICKETS.

6. Tickets for places on the North London Railway where no station is specified and the fare is uniform, are available only for stations between Chalk Farm, Camden Road, and Broad Street (City), or between Kingsland and Bow, respectively. Holders of these tickets proceeding to places beyond the stations above-named, will be required to pay (in addition to any payment already made) the local fare from the nearest of the above points, to the station at which they alight.

7. Tickets, unless otherwise specified, are only available by trains travelling direct to the stations for which they are issued.

8. Collectors must be careful if all cases to tear off, on completion of the first journey, the *right-hand* portion of return tickets.

9. Tickets, unless otherwise specified, are only available for the day of issue; ...".

This quotation excludes the section dealing with tickets beyond Bow; these will be dealt with in Chapter Six. A few comments are necessary; the "Ordinary Tickets" of paragraph 1 are ordinary singles and respective halves of ordinary returns. The colour "Red" for 2nd class by down trains would perhaps more accurately have been described as pink, but the official company designation is used throughout this work.

Poplar station was not yet open. The official name of Highbury was Islington or Highbury and it was still shown on tickets as Islington. Short Journey tickets from Camden Road to Chalk Farm and to Caledonian Road carried the number 2, those to Kentish Town the letter A. The "ordinary colours" of the Bow-City tickets of paragraph 2 were determined in relation to the base colour on the City Extension, i.e. tickets towards Broad Street were yellow with a white stripe and blue with a red stripe respectively, those away from Broad Street were white with a yellow stripe and red with a blue stripe.

This Order was obviously expected to come into force forthwith, as otherwise Kingsland would not have been included in the number allocation. Indeed the system of numbers and letters for Short Journey tickets was probably already in operation, reduced fares for such journeys having been established from 1 January 1864.

Paragraph 6 suggests the continuance of flat fare tickets, available on the basis of two zones rather than over the whole of the system as before. It is not known whether in fact any of these were ever used. If they were, then on the basis of Minutes dated 2 April 1872 such use had been discontinued by June 1868. Those Minutes give an analysis of ordinary passenger traffic between Broad Street and Caledonian Road, Islington and Newington Road for the half years ending 30 June 1868 to 31 December 1871. In each case an exact cash figure is given. As the fares to all three stations were equal this would only have been possible by analysis of ticket issue at Broad Street, which in turn supposes separate station to station tickets for each of the three destinations.

What is clear is that on the opening of the City Extension

station to station single tickets fell into two categories, ordinary and Short Journey. Short Journey tickets were First and Second Class only, station to station tickets were First, Second and Third Class, the last were only issued for the one Parliamentary train each way per day. Returns were First and Second Class only, it is not thought that there were any Short Journey returns as the fare tables for December 1865 and January 1866 only show single ticket fares for Short Journeys, the return ticket fares column is blank.

The December 1865 timetable shows three local services. Trains ran between Chalk Farm and Broad Street every fifteen minutes at the even quarter, on weekdays leaving Chalk Farm from 7.00 a.m. until 10.30 p.m. and leaving Broad Street from 7.15 a.m. until 10.45 p.m. Third Class passengers were conveyed by the 7.00 a.m. from Chalk Farm and the 7.00 p.m. from Broad Street. Trains from Broad Street to Kew ran every half hour from 7.25 a.m. until 9.55 p.m., calling at Shoreditch, Dalston Junction, Camden Road, all HJR stations, Acton and Kew. No through trains for Third Class bookings are shown, but there must have been one each way conveying passengers between HJR and N&SWJR stations in order to meet statutory requirements. From 1 February 1868 the Shoreditch stop was replaced by one at Islington.

Trains between Broad Street and Fenchurch Street ran every fifteen minutes leaving Broad Street from 7.37 a.m. until 9.22 p.m. and leaving Fenchurch Street from 8.15 a.m. until 10.00 p.m. There were also earlier and later "local" trains between Broad Street and Bow and vice-versa. Third Class passengers were carried by the 6.45 a.m. from Bow to Broad Street and by the 7.07 p.m. from Broad Street as far as Bow only.

ORDINARY LOCAL TICKETS 1865 - 1873

To assist cross-reference tickets supplied by Waterlow from 1 July 1865 will be given Type references. The first Waterlow tickets were untitled, the standard station to station single format being as shown in Figures 16 to 18. This is designated as Type LOS1, the conditions notice (which was to remain standard until 1912) was already in use, it has been seen on a foreign Edmondson print (see Figure 139). The Figure 16 ticket is a red unidirectional issue from an NLR station, corresponding tickets from HJR and N&SWJR stations were in identical format. The Figure 17 ticket is for a down/up bi-directional journey, it shows a departure from G.O.32 in that the stripe on the white background is red rather than yellow. This may have been an early change of practice, later white and yellow bi-directional singles also carried a red stripe although returns appear always to have used the yellow and white combinations given in the Order. Bi-directional tickets of later Types are illustrated in Plate 1.

Figure 16

G.O.32 and indicates that by 1872 the colours of 3rd class tickets had been reversed, buff becoming the standard up colour and green the standard down colour. Borley states that this change occurred in 1875, but this ticket is clear evidence of an earlier date.

Figure 17

Figure 18

The standard format for the contemporary Short Journey tickets is shown in Figure 19 (Type LOS1SJ), note that in addition to the longitudinal stripe and distinguishing number or letter there is also a notice "Available between the above Stations only." The number or letter also appears on the back of the ticket, which is coloured the same as the front, red with a white stripe. Again, the ticket of Figure 19 is from an NLR station and corresponding tickets from HJR and N&SWJR stations have been seen. Figure 20 shows a slightly later N&SWJR ticket on plain red card, issued in 1868, clearly the longitudinal stripes on Short Journey tickets were very soon discontinued. Again, the station letter also appears on the back.

Figure 19

Figure 20

Figure 18 shows a Third Class issue from an HJR station, with the two black transverse stripes referred to in paragraph 1 of G.O.32. These would almost certainly have been printed to indicate availability in the second class carriages, the number of stripes was a commonly used class indicator. The ticket is for an up journey and is buff, it thus conflicts with

The return half of a corresponding ordinary return is shown in Figure 21 (Type LOR1). Note that in accordance with paragraph 6 of the Collection of Tickets section of G.O.32 it is marked "Change at Dalston Junc." It is also marked "Not available beyond" immediately below Bow. These additional notices, of course, only appeared when required. This blue

Plate 1: Bi-directional tickets

Plate 2: Singles to Acton GWR

Plate 3: Singles to Kensington

return half is for a wholly up journey (Caledonian Rd - Dalston then Dalston - Bow), the outward half would have been red.

Figure 21

Shortly after Type LOR1 was introduced the notice "Not transferable" was added to the return half only to give Type LOR2, illustrated by the non-matching halves of Figure 22. The yellow return half is dated January 1867, the date on the white outward half is illegible.

Figure 22

Only First and Second class return tickets were issued, there were no Third class. As already stated, no Short Journey return fares are given in the January 1866 timetable, but in the January 1870 timetable they are shown between adjacent stations on the City Extension and between adjacent stations on the Bow line, which by then had been extended to Poplar. None were given for Main Line, HJR or N&SWJR stations except for Kentish Town - Camden Road but not vice versa. In the October 1870 timetable Short Journey return fares are given for all pairs of adjacent stations. It is not known whether Type LOR1 had a corresponding Short Journey type, but Type LOR2 did and a first class example on yellow card is shown in Figure 23 (Type LOR2SJ). The station code letters appear on the front and back of each half.

Figure 23

The next development was to abandon anonymity and to show the company title on tickets. Titled tickets are known from an earliest issue date of February 1870, a yellow Short Journey NLR issue is shown in Figure 24 (Type LOS2SJ), the station number is repeated on the back. By October 1870 miniature repeats of the destination station had been added at each side of the foot of the ticket to give Types LOS3 and LOS3SJ, illustrated in Figures 25 to 28. Children under 12 years of age travelled at half-price. Specially printed child tickets seem to have been rarely used, and each child travelling on a single journey would usually be issued with half of a vertically bisected adult ticket. The miniature repeats ensured that each half showed the destination in full.

Figure 24

Figure 25 shows an up NLR buff Third Class ticket with black transverse stripes, note that on this later issue (c/f Figure 18) the abbreviation "PARLY" also appears, making it clear that the fare only applied to Parliamentary trains. Figures 26 to 28 show Short Journey issues, pink from the NLR and blue from the HJR and N&SWJR, the station codes are repeated on the backs. The NLR title was shown either as "N.L.R." or "N.L.Ry.", the two forms were contemporary. Equally well, there is no date implication in the fact that the miniature repeats were shown in either lower or upper case (the former is commoner but upper case repeats frequently occur) or that the class was printed in either upper (more common) or lower case.

Figure 25

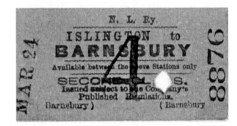

Figure 26

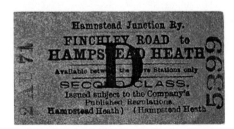

Figure 27

Figure 28

Miniature repeats were not used on local ordinary returns, which were diagonally bisected from bottom left to top right for child issue, and thus one type of return was contemporary with both single Types LOS2 and LOS3. The Type did, however, appear in two versions, a first version as shown in Figure 29 (a white/yellow Type LOR3b) with the conditions notice at the bottom of each half and a second version as shown in Figure 30 (non-matching white outward and yellow return halves of Short Journey tickets, Type LOR3tSJ) with this notice at the bottom of the outward half and the top of the return half. "Not transferable" appears on the return half only, above the conditions if these are at the bottom of the half and either above or below the conditions if these are at the top.

Figure 29

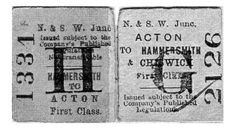

Figure 30

A study of many specimens has led to the tentative conclusion that all the earliest tickets of this type had conditions at the bottom of the return half, as on the immediately preceding Type LOR2. Shortly thereafter, however, practice appears to have changed, with bottom conditions (Type LOR3b) being used on:

a) tickets from Broad Street to any other NLR station,
b) tickets from any NLR station to Broad Street, and
c) tickets between any two City Extension stations.

Conditions were shown at the top of the return half (Type LOR3t) on:

d) tickets between any two NLR stations other than in (a) to (c) above,
e) tickets from Broad Street to any HJR or N&SWJR station,
f) tickets between any two N&SWJR stations,
g) tickets from N&SWJR stations to Broad Street.

No tickets from the N&SWJR to HJR stations or to NLR stations other than Broad Street have been seen, nor have any contemporary HJR titled tickets.

During the period from 1865 to 1873 there were a number of station changes as follows:-

Victoria Park re-sited on 1 March 1866.
Kentish Town renamed Gospel Oak on 1 February 1867.
Caledonian Road renamed Barnsbury on 1 July 1870 and re-sited on 21 November 1870.
Newington Road renamed Canonbury on 1 July 1870 and re-sited on 1 December 1870.
Camden Road renamed Camden Town on 1 July 1870 and re-sited on 5 December 1870.

Hackney re-sited on 1 December 1870.
Edgeware Road renamed Edgware Road & Brondesbury from 1 January 1872 and then Brondesbury (Edgware Road) from 1 January 1873.
Islington or Highbury renamed Highbury & Islington on 1 July 1872.

The Edgeware Road changes are as given by Borley; note, however, that the ticket of Figure 18 simply shows Edgeware Road. Some tickets printed after July 1872 show the incorrect name "Islington & Highbury". None of the above changes affected the code number or letter, which was simply retained by the renamed or re-sited station. Kew finally closed some time in 1866, it had been little used since January 1862 and despite the code listing in G.O.32 the only tickets seen with the letter K involve Kew Bridge, not Kew.

New stations that opened did, however, require new code letters; the dates and allocations (so far as known) were as follows:

Poplar	1 August 1866	**P**
(code already allocated in G.O.32)		
Willesden Junction	1 September 1866	**W**
Kentish Town	1 April 1867	?
*(code **B** may have transferred from the old Kentish Town station renamed Gospel Oak on the same day, with Gospel Oak receiving a new code)*		
Old Ford	1 July 1867	?
Haggerston	2 September 1867	**X**
Homerton	1 October 1868	?
Blackwall	1 September 1870	?
(for NLR trains)		
Kensal Green	1 July 1873	?
*(code **F** may have transferred from Kensal Green & Harlesden, closed the same day)*		

A further development was the opening of the L&SWR Richmond Extension line from South Acton to Richmond New Station on 1 January 1869, there were intermediate stations at Brentford Road (renamed Gunnersbury on 1 November 1871) and Kew Gardens. From this date most trains over the N&SWJR ran either to Richmond or to Kew Bridge. Staff were warned by General Order No 65 that care must be taken that tickets for Kew Bridge, Brentford Road, Kew Gardens and Richmond are issued for the proper trains. Tickets between Extension line stations were standard L&SWR prints and thus outside the scope of this work, tickets from those stations to South Acton and beyond were N&SWJ titled and were in local format if to a N&SWJR, HJR or NLR station. Special NLR booking offices were provided at Richmond until 1917 and Kew Bridge until 1 July 1918. Tickets from NLR and N&SWJR stations to Extension line stations were also in local format.

One other event from this period was to have a major affect on subsequent ticket practice - the HJR was absorbed by the L&NWR on 15 July 1867. Working by the NLR continued until 30 June 1872 after which the NLR had full running powers. Tickets to HJR stations after this date will be dealt with in Chapter Nine.

FARES AND CLASSES 1866-1875

Shown on the next page is the fare table for tickets between NLR stations and from NLR to L&BR stations as given in the January 1866 timetable. The underlying flat fare structure, modified by Short Journey fares between adjacent stations is clear (the missing figure at the foot of the 2nd class return column should be 6). There are two exceptions to this, the higher fares (as would be expected) to L&BR stations east of

NORTH LONDON RAILWAY.

FARES.

BETWEEN		SINGLE JOURNEY.			RETURN TICKETS.	
		1st Class.	2nd Class.	3rd Class.	1st Class.	2nd Class.
		s. d.	s. d.	s. d.	s. d.	s. d.
Chalk Farm, Camden Road, Caledonian Road, or Islington	And Broad Street, Shoreditch, or Dalston Junction.	0 6	0 4	0 3	0 9	0 6
Newington Road	„ Do. do.	0 6	0 4	0 2	0 9	0 6
Dalston Junction	„ Broad Street	0 4	0 3	0 1	0 6	0 4
Shoreditch	„ Do.	0 3	0 2	0 1	...	...
Bow or Victoria Park	„ Do.	0 6	0 4	0 3	0 9	0 6
Hackney	„ Do.	0 6	0 4	0 2	0 9	0 6
Chalk Farm, Camden Road, Caledonian Road, Islington, Newington Road, or Dalston Junction	„ Bow, Victoria Park, or Hackney	0 6	0 4	0 3	0 9	0 6
Do. do.	„ Stepney, Shadwell, or Fenchurch Street	0 6	0 4	...	0 9	0 6
Do. do.	„ Blackwall and Stations east of Stepney	0 8	0 6	...	1 0	0 9
Any Station on North London Railway	„ The Station next to it in each direction	0 3	0 2	0 1	...	...
Any Station on North London Railway	„ Any Station other than above named	0 6	0 4	...	0 9	0

Tickets, unless otherwise specified thereon, are only available to the Stations for which they are issued. Passengers proceeding beyond the Station for which their Tickets are taken, will be required to pay the Local Fare between the Station to which they were booked and that at which they alight.

RETURN TICKETS, unless otherwise specified, are only available for the day on which they are issued, and to and from the Stations named thereon.

Stepney and the lower fares between Dalston Junction and Broad Street. The third class fares, available only by one train each way per day, are generally below the Parliamentary rate of 1d per mile. The inevitable dismantling of this structure was a process of evolution rather than revolution and the following account is based mainly on company Minutes, particularly those of the Locomotive Stores & Traffic Committee (referred to hereafter as the LS&TC).

On 16 August 1866 a meeting was held with officers of the L&NWR over that company's intent to open Broad Street for a portion of their main line traffic north of Willesden from 1 September 1866, to close their old Willesden station and open a new Willesden Junction station with upper and lower level platforms. As will be seen in Chapter Ten the agreed fares reflected the NLR flat fare structure. On 3 September 1867 the L&NWR commenced a through service between Kensington and Broad Street; they agreed with the NLR that all trains would be first and second class only and fares were again based on NLR flat fares.

In November 1869 it was reported that there had been a falling off of passenger traffic receipts from Bow, Old Ford and Victoria Park to Fenchurch Street; also that traffic from Highbury to Broad Street had suffered in view of the Great Northern Railway's frequent service from Holloway to Moorgate Street at a 3rd class fare of 3d for the single journey. These are the first intimations that the lack of third class accommodation by all trains was beginning to hurt the NLR.

Borley states that commencing 1 September 1870 the fares between adjacent stations, i.e. for the Short Journey tickets, were reduced to 2d first class and 1d second class, and that this necessitated modifications to other short distance fares. This appears to be an over-simplification, a comparison between fare tables for January and October 1870 does reveal such 2d and 1d fares in the latter but only in 11 out of 23 possible station pairs and only when the journey was not more than one mile (but not in all such cases). When these low fares do appear then no third class fare is quoted.

The N&SWJR was leased by the LNWR, NLR and Midland Railway effective from 1 January 1871. At a meeting to review the lease, held on 11 May 1871, the NLR issue of first and second class tickets only was discussed, Mr Mansel stating his view that the issue of third class tickets would diminish the receipts and require the building of additional second class carriages. Later in May the issue of first and second class only was discussed internally. If third class were to be adopted it was estimated that instead of 216 second class carriages the requirement would be for 110 second class and 125 third class and that it would be necessary to construct 19 standard second class carriages and convert 125 to third class. The subject was referred to the Board for further consideration.

On 19 March 1872 a meeting with the L&NWR considered the question of booking third class passengers between Kensington and Broad Street. The NLR stated that they were not in a position to enter into any general arrangement for third class bookings to and from the West London Railway except between such stations as are served by L&NWR trains, the NLR not being provided with third class carriages. Furthermore, such carriages would prejudice the question of Railway Passenger Duty then under consideration with the Board of Inland Revenue. This was significant; under the Railway Regulation Act of 1844 the Board of Trade had been given powers to dispense with certain of the conditions relating to travel at the 1d per mile Parliamentary fare, and had in fact relaxed the requirement that such trains must stop at every station. It will be recalled that in 1858 all the company's trains had been approved as Parliamentary Trains when the actual fare paid did not exceed 1d per mile; this view also applied to the many fast trains which did not stop at all stations. In 1866, however, the Board of Trade was advised that it did not in fact have the power to dispense with the stoppage requirement. This was challenged by the railway companies, the Board of Inland Revenue brought an action against the NLR as a test case and the Court of Exchequer decided in the Revenue's favour on 6 July 1874 (Charles E. Lee - *Passenger Class Distinctions*).

From 1 May 1873 first and second class single and return fares between stations west of Dalston and Burdett Road, Stepney, Shadwell, Fenchurch Street and Blackwall were increased (in some cases by 50%!), as were the same range of flat fares between Kew Bridge and stations Hackney to Poplar. In October 1873 the Manager was asked to consider and report on modification of Shoreditch, Dalston and Hackney fares (but not to Broad Street) in view of tram competition.

On 6 October 1874 it was recommended to the Board that the ordinary fares between Canonbury and Broad Street (a distance of 3 miles) be revised as follows:

	Present Ordinary Fares	Proposed Fares
1st day (return)	9d	8d
2nd day (return)	6d	5d
1st single	6d	5d
2nd single	4d	3d

Note that the existing fares were still the original flat fares, the new fares (second class at the Parliamentary rate but higher than the then ruling third class fare of 2½d) were adopted from 1 November 1874. There was also a suggestion that the Dalston - Broad Street second class single fare be reduced from 3d (higher than the Parliamentary rate but less than the flat fare) to 2d to meet tramway competition, it would also entitle a claim to exemption from Passenger Duty; this change was, however, deferred.

Pressure to introduce 3rd class was obviously increasing and indeed NLR three-class trains commenced running through to the Great Northen Railway in January 1875 (see Chapter 10). The dispute with the Revenue having been settled, and a clear direction as to the law given, the final straw was an announcement by the Midland Railway, which had abolished second class on the whole of its system from 1 January 1875, that they were to introduce a Moorgate Street - Richmond service via the N&SWJR on 1 July 1875. A meeting of NLR officers on 26 July 1875 considered the Midland rates and resolved to recommend that on and from 1 August third class carriages be attached to the NLR trains forming the Kew and Richmond service, the first and second class rates to remain as at present, and the third class fares to be the same as charged by the Midland Company; and that third class fares be quoted for intermediate stations on the Hampstead Junction line, as at present by the Mansion House service of the L&NWR.

This inevitably opened the possibility of third class travel between those NLR stations at which the fast trains stopped, and such bookings were indeed allowed, except between Dalston and Broad Street during the hours of 8.00 and 10.00 a.m. and 4.00 and 6.00 p.m.

The attention of the meeting was also called to the fact that between Kensington and Broad Street first and second class fares only were in force, whilst third class rates were adopted via the Metropolitan route. Mr Mansel explained that there was no objection on the part of the NLR to third class bookings being adopted between Broad Street and Kensington, but pointed out that having regard to the uniform fare between Kensington and intermediate stations between Broad Street and Willesden, any reduction of fare would be followed by a considerable loss and urged that the present third class rates should not be less than 6d, and a second class quoted intermediate between that sum and the charge of 9d first class.

A Minute of 14 September 1875 records that a number of carriages were then in the course of alteration to meet the proposed third class arrangements. On 5 October 1875 the Manager reported to the Locomotive Stores & Traffic Committee that third class bookings between all stations had been adopted from the 1st of that month, that one third class carriage had been attached to each train and that on 1 November a sufficient number of carriages will have been converted to allow a second such carriage. This was duly achieved, and third class return tickets were then put into operation. The accounts for the half year to 31 December 1875 include the item:

" Printing, stationery and tickets. Increase £379 - new ticket cases and supply of 3rd class tickets. Government duty decrease £886 due to exemption in respect of passengers carried at 3rd class fares by stopping trains. Carriages wages increase £345 due to conversion of 2nd class into 3rd."

Ironically, the Midland service was unsuccessful and it was withdrawn on 1 February 1876.

Thus, the second half of 1875 saw the general introduction of third class singles at 1d per mile and of third class returns. The earlier types of third class tickets required for Parliamentary bookings were presumably withdrawn. This is in accord with Borley, who says that in 1875 third class tickets were issued between all stations, he adds that for a few months between many adjacent stations both the second and third class fares were 1d, but later second class was raised to 1½d. With this exception the second class fares remained unaltered, the new third class being in general a little lower.

The new arrangements prompted the company to appoint two Travelling Ticket Inspectors as the necessity for checking tickets had been "considerably increased". Returns show that they were effective in collecting significant amounts of excess fares, and they later reported substantial improper use of the second halves of return tickets from stations at a 2d fare, the price of two single tickets. As a result of this, 2d returns were discontinued from April 1882.

Chapter Five

NLR and N&SWJR
ORDINARY LOCAL TICKETS 1873-1912

In November 1873 there was a very significant change in ticket practice throughout the system. General Order No 115, issued in that month, reads as follows:

"In order to give greater facility to Collectors and Examiners in detecting tickets which are chargeable with excess, in case of passengers travelling beyond the stations for which they are booked, all tickets supplied in future to the stations to replace the present stock as expended, will bear on the front the number of the station to which they are issued.

The Stations will be numbered as under, viz.:-

1	Broad Street	16	Blackwall
2	Shoreditch	17	Kentish Town
3	Haggerston	18	Gospel Oak
4	Dalston Junction	19	Hampstead Heath
5	Canonbury	20	Finchley Road
6	Highbury	21	Edgware Road
7	Barnsbury	22	Kensal Green
8	Camden Town	23	Willesden Junction
9	Chalk Farm	24	Acton
10	Hackney	25	Hammersmith
11	Homerton	26	Kew Bridge
12	Victoria Park	27	Gunnersbury
13	Old Ford	28	Kew Gardens
14	Bow	29	Richmond
15	Poplar		

The numbers and initials on the present Local tickets will be discontinued, and the numbers as above substituted.

The tickets issued *from* stations on the Hampstead Junction line will not at present be numbered."

From this it can be assumed that special Short Journey tickets (referred to as "Local tickets" in the Order) were discontinued. Stocks of ordinary tickets would thus have been simplified to first and second class station to station singles and returns, together with 3rd class station to station singles for Parliamentary fare journeys. The Order does not mention colours, but tickets show that the existing colours for unidirectional singles of up yellow, blue and buff with two black stripes and down white, red and green with two black stripes continued. Striped bi-directional singles and bi-coloured returns also continued as before.

Figures 31 and 32 show respectively a yellow Type LOS4 single and non-matching halves of a white/yellow Type LOR4t return as introduced from November 1873. The latter has the return half conditions clause at the top of the return half, for the journeys specified in Chapter 4 there was also a version with this clause at the bottom, Type LOR4b. The basic formats are the same as for Types LOS3, LOR3t and LOR3b, but the new station numbers have been added. As with the earlier types the North London title was shown as either N.L.R. or N.L.Ry. and the class and miniature repeats on singles were in either upper or lower case.

Figure 31

Figure 32

The next change to occur was a natural result of the upheavals in the fare structure, the addition of the fare to the right of the class to give Types LOS5, LOR5b and LOR5t. Again, the title was either N.L.R. or N.L.Ry. and the class and miniature repeats on singles were in either upper or lower case. The earliest issue date seen for Type LOS5 is 24 April 1875. At this time it was very unusual for fares to be printed on tickets, legislation only made it compulsory from 1 July 1890, and indeed the NLR appears to have been the only company to do this as a matter of course. No doubt it was a wise move, the scope for passenger confusion and complaint must have been considerable during this transitional period.

Three singles of Type LOS5 are shown in Figures 33 to 35, all for the same journey and forming a very interesting group. Figure 33 shows a second class issue between adjacent stations, conforming to the colour scheme set out in G.O.32, blue being the up colour and the red stripe marking the ticket as bi-directional. The journey is between adjacent stations and confirms that Short Journey tickets were no longer in use. Figure 34 shows a buff third class issue (note the "PARLY" designation has been omitted - c/f Figure 25), the issue date appears to be 8 October 1875 and the two stripes indicate that when the ticket was printed the intent was to carry the third class passenger in a second class carriage. Figure 35 shows a later ordinary third class issue, dated 16 November 1875 and on plain buff card. The lack of transverse stripes indicates

Figure 33

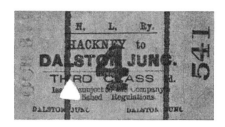

Figure 34

Figure 35

that a second class carriage would not then have been used, showing that third class carriages were by then working on the Bow line. This ticket evidence is consistent with the Minute book statement that third class passengers were conveyed by all trains from 1 October 1875.

The lack of a green stripe on the tickets of Figures 34 and 35 ticket is noticeable. From the former it is assumed that while black stripes were used on third class tickets they took precedence (as may be expected) over the single stripe that would otherwise have been required as a bi-directional marking. Figure 35, together with a plain buff return half from Old Ford to Broad Street dated January 1886, and a plain buff single from Bow to Dalston Junction dated May 1888 suggest that it may in fact have been some time before striped card was used for bi-directional third class tickets; April 1888 is the earliest date seen for such a print.

Figure 36 shows a white/yellow contemporary return with conditions at the top of the return half, Type LOR5t; there was also a Type LOR5b with conditions at the bottom of the return half. Note that the presence of the fare necessitated an abbreviation of the class. The North London title appeared as either N.L.R. or N.L.Ry., and "Return" was shown in either lower or upper case, neither variation had date significance. As has been seen, the fare was usually printed on tickets from mid-1875, prior to the general use of third class. It must be

mentioned, however, that during a short transitional period some third class singles on plain card (without the two black transverse stripes) and some third class returns appeared without the fare, in Types LOS4, LOR4t and LOR4b respectively.

Types LOS5, LOR5t and LOR5b remained current until 1880. Godfrey Croughton (*Transport Ticket Society Journal* September 1994, page 337) drew attention to the single capital letters that appeared on NLR tickets from that year. Tickets bearing these letters are considered to be distinct Types LOS6 and LOR6b illustrated in Figure 37 (green, note the letter K to the left of the lower line of the conditions notice) and Figure 38 (red/blue, note the letters G at the centre of the ticket). There were also some Type LOR6t returns with conditions at the top of the return half, but these seem to have been short-lived and conditions at the bottom of the return half then became standard for all journeys. The North London title appears to have been shown uniformly as N.L.R. on this and all subsequent types, but the class and miniature repeats could still be found in either upper or lower case.

It is worth reproducing the table that Croughton prepared, indeed the opportunity has been taken of updating it to take account of a further 800 tickets that have been examined.

Code Letter	Number of Examples	Earliest Date	Latest *Common* Date	Latest Date
&	7	02.1880	1885	06.1890
A	95	04.1885	1912	12.1937
B	8	03.1908	1908	06.1912
D	2	03.1895	1897	10.1897
E	3	1909	1909	05.1911
F	440	1889	1908	01.1917
G	112	04.1880	1898	09.1903
H	9	03.1898	1908	01.1911
I	1	03.1912	1912	03.1912
K	720	07.1880	1912	04.1935
L	6	01.1882	1895	02.1895
N	19	11.1888	1912	08.1912
O	141	09.1880	1905	07.1915
P	2	1892	1902	09.1902
R	14	04.1881	1902	12.1902
S	9	08.1890	1906	04.1906
T	1	10.1892	1892	10.1892
U	1	06.1906	1906	06.1906
V	10	188?	1894	10.1903
W	24	04.1893	1896	1912
X	3	07.1883	1897	10.1897
Y	3	08.1888	1895	02.1895
Z	7	06.1888	1897	09.1902

He suggested that the preponderance of K and F and the total absence of some letters of the alphabet (C, J, M and Q, but most notably C) indicated that these were not series letters. This appears to be clearly correct, series were in fact indicated by a series number, the tickets of Figures 37 and 38 both show S.2 -Series 2. He also posited that they may have been

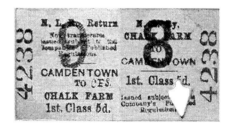

Figure 36

Figure 37

Figure 38

intended to identify the clerk who authorised the printing or the compositor who set up the type. Similar letters or printcodes as they may be termed also appear on many Metropolitan and Metropolitan District Railway tickets, which were also printed by Waterlow.

Type LOS6 was printed until about 1888; by April in that year there had been a further change in ordinary singles, to Type LOS7 with the fare to each side of the class as shown in Figures 39 and 40, both buff. The corresponding change on returns was to move the fare to the left of the class on the return half as shown in Figure 41, a buff/green Type LOR7. This may have occurred at the same time as the format for singles was changed or it could have been slightly later, the earliest issue date seen is 4 April 1891. It will be seen that both changes ensured that the fare was shown on each half of a vertically bisected single ticket and of a return ticket bisected diagonally from bottom left to top right. The ticket of Figure 39 carries the N&SW Junc title in the abbreviated form used from Types LOS4 and LOR4 onwards, until at some time during the 1890s there was a change to a title wholly in initials as shown in Figure 40.

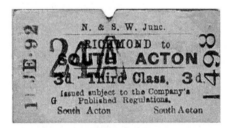

Figure 39

Figure 40

Figure 41

By May 1897 the availability had been added below the title to give Type LOS8 (Figure 42, red) and Type LOR8 (Figure 43,

Figure 42

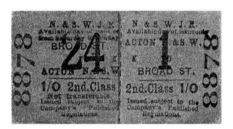

Figure 43

red/blue). In July 1902 letters from the London County Council and the Metropolitan Borough Councils were submitted to the Board, urging an extension of the time of availability of ordinary return tickets. The Manager reported to the Board that it had been agreed that, as from 1 August 1902, return tickets will be available on the day following that of issue. The availability shown on local return halves changed accordingly to give Type LOR9 (Figure 44, yellow/white). The change was announced by an amendment dated 28 July 1902 to General Order No 188, which also indicated that exceptions to local two day availability would be tickets from NLR stations to Kew Gardens and Richmond, and N&SWJR tickets for the reverse journeys, for which the return availability was to be four days (Figure 45, buff).

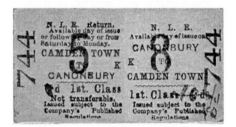

Figure 44

Figure 45

By January 1906 use was being made of single and return tickets available to any one of a number of alternative destinations at the same fare. Originally at least some of these carried the number of the furthest distant station, Types LOS9 and LOR10 shown in Figures 46 (buff) and 47 (white/yellow). Later, it was realised that station numbers on alternative destination tickets were a nonsense and they were then omitted to give Types LOS10 and LOR11 shown in Figures 48 (green) and 49 (yellow/white). One known destination group was Shoreditch and Broad Street, both on

Figure 46

Figure 47

Figure 48

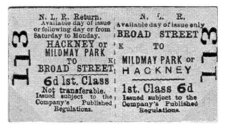

Figure 49

Figure 50

Figure 51

but tickets printed by the L&NWR were to come into use from 1 July 1912 as will be seen in Chapter Eleven.

Changes in station names from 1873 were as follows:

Hammersmith was renamed Hammersmith & Chiswick on 1 July 1880.
Barnsbury was renamed Caledonian Road & Barnsbury on 22 May 1893.
Finchley Road (St Johns Wood) became Finchley Road & Frognal on 1 October 1880.
Brondesbury (Edgware Rd) became Brondesbury on 1 May 1883.
Kensal Green became Kensal Rise on 24 May 1890.

The date of the name change for Hammersmith is that given by Borley and indeed all studied company timetable and other documents prior to that date do simply show Hammersmith. It is noteworthy, however, that many tickets of the 1870s show Hammersmith & Chiswick (or Hammersmith or Chiswick!) as the destination, even though the departure station is only shown as Hammersmith. It should also be mentioned that after Great Western Railway trains started running to Willesden in January 1888 Acton was always shown as Acton (N&SW) to distinguish it from the GWR station. Station name changes did not affect the station codes. Neither was ticket practice affected when new L&NWR connections between the HJR and the N&SWJR at Willesden were opened, together with new platforms, on 20 July 1885.

As new stations were opened they were given the number of the lower-numbered adjacent station, with a suffix A, as follows:

Mildmay Park	1 January 1880	**4A**
South Acton	1 January 1880	**24A**
South Bromley	1 September 1884	**14A**
Maiden Lane	1 July 1887	**7A**
West End Lane	1 March 1888	**20A**
Brondesbury Park	1 September 1908	**21A (?)**

LS&TC Minutes show that Maiden Lane was supplied with three ticket cases containing 1108 tubes.

In addition code 10A was allocated to Hackney No. 2. Hackney Downs (Great Eastern Railway) and the west end of the platforms at Hackney (NLR) were linked by covered footways from 1 December 1885; Hackney No. 2 office was on these footways, an LS&TC Minute dated 30 July 1890 refers to a requisition by the audit clerk for a ticket case for *"the interchange office at Hackney"*.

the City Extension line. Tickets from Bow line stations to this group were in bi-directional colours. Otherwise singles and outward halves of returns when all destinations were up, whether NLR or N&SWJR titled were yellow, blue and buff. White, red and green cards were used for NLR singles and outward halves to down destinations or for any combination of down, up and bi-directional journeys and for N&SWJR singles and outward halves to down destinations. Return halves were the opposite colours to the outward halves.

Dalston Junction station issued 1d third class singles to Highbury & Islington, Homerton or Shoreditch and 2d third class returns to Highbury & Islington, Homerton or Broad Street from automatic pull-bar machines, the purchase of which was authorised in July 1910. Two machines were used for returns, distinguished by A.I. No 1 and A.I. No 2 on the tickets. Figures 50 and 51 show examples of these, both tickets are plain green; note that the usual series number has been replaced by a series letter.

Types LOS8 and LOR9 (and LOS10 and LOR11 where appropriate) then continued in use until 1912. They remained unaffected by the events of February 1909 when common management of the NLR with the L&NWR came into force,

As Figures 52 (yellow) and 53 (red/blue) show the suffix was usually in the form of a capital A, but for Mildmay Park 4a has been seen on tickets dated April 1883 (Figure 54, green) and December 1885, 4A dated 16 February 1891. All the suffixed codes have been seen on tickets except 21A, and with this exception all codes were included in a new list issued as General Order No 390 dated 30 September 1904. Indeed, 21A may not have been allocated, as alternative destination tickets were in use by the opening date of Brondesbury Park and its proximity to the adjacent stations at Brondesbury and Kensal Rise would have made a natural destination group.

Figure 52

Figure 53

Figure 54

THE HAMMERSMITH BRANCH

Hammersmith was initially treated in the same way as any other N&SWJR station for ticketing purposes. Early working was either by a dropped carriage as already mentioned or by an engine propelling the train from Acton to the trailing junction and then reversing to run down along the branch. From 1 November 1865 only the latter practice was operated. In the 1860s and 1870s no fares were quoted between Hammersmith and Kew Bridge or any station on the Richmond Extension line.

South Acton station opened on 1 January 1880 and from that date, a shuttle service operated from there to Hammersmith. During the period of the shuttle service tickets between Hammersmith and stations beyond South Acton carried the instruction "Change at South Acton" (Figure 55, red/blue).

From 8 April 1909 the branch was served by a rail motor car and three new halts were opened - at Rugby Road, Woodstock Road and Bath Road. The rail motor also served Kew Bridge, which became less important from 1909 onwards, with nearly all Broad Street trains running to Richmond. Buff multiple

Figure 55

destination single and return edmondsons as shown in Figures 56 and 57 were issued at the booking offices at Kew Bridge, Acton and South Acton, while ticket issue on the branch was on the cars. Officers' Committee Minutes record that Hammersmith booking office closed on and from 8 April 1909 and that through bookings with stations north, east and south of Willesden were abolished.

Initially thin card tickets were used on the rail motors (white with a red overprint) as shown in Figure 58, later edmondsons (green with a red overprint) as shown in Figure 59. Both these tickets were printed by the L&NWR, the former has conditions J1 on the back and the latter conditions J2.

Figure 56

Figure 57

Figure 58

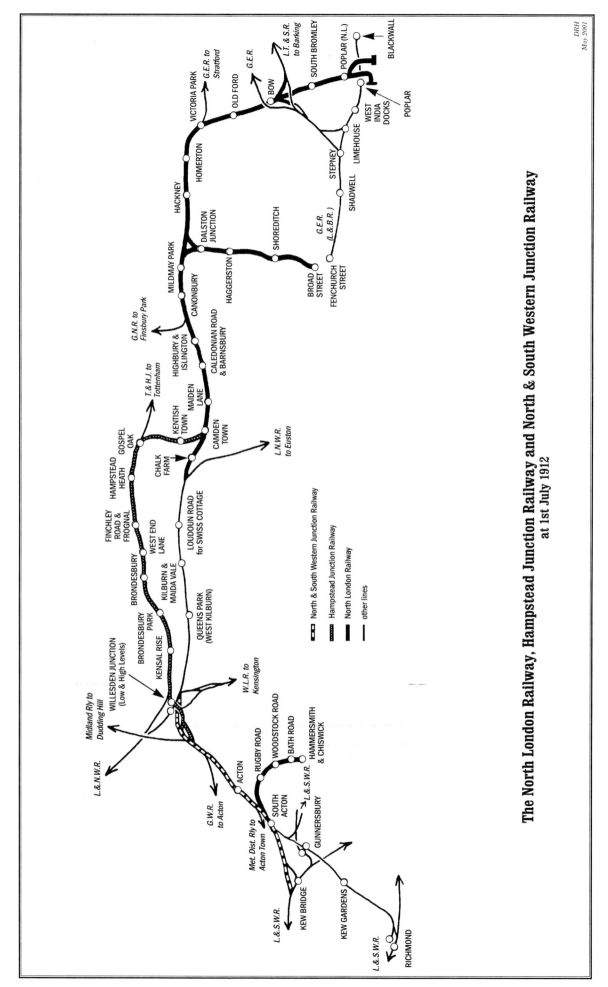

The North London Railway, Hampstead Junction Railway and North & South Western Junction Railway
at 1st July 1912

Figure 59

Never popular with passengers (indeed the NLR gave notice to discontinue the service from 31 December 1872 but relented later in the year), the branch continued to decline and the passenger service ceased on 1 January 1917.

ঙ্গC৪

Chapter Six

LOCAL TICKETS BEYOND BOW 1865-1870

General Order No. 32 deals with bookings to and from L&BR stations from September 1865 as follows:

"3. Tickets between North London Stations, and Stepney, Shadwell, and Fenchurch Street are distinguished by a broad *transverse* stripe as under:-

	UP TICKETS		DOWN TICKETS	
	Colour / Stripe		Colour / Stripe	
First Class	Yellow	Red	White	Red
Second Class	Blue	White	Red	White

These Tickets are not available for Stations on the City Extension Line (excepting Dalston Junction), nor at Stations east of Bow Junction.

4. Tickets for Stations east of Stepney Junction are distinguished by a broad Brown *transverse* stripe, and are not available at Stations on the City Extension line (excepting Dalston Junction)."

Up tickets were those towards Fenchurch Street.

The return half shown in Figure 60 is plain blue and thus pre-dates the issue of G.O.32., it was probably issued at Fenchurch Street. It covers a flat fare booking to any NLR station and differs from the standard local Type LOR1 by having the class at the top and also by showing the fare, the actual figure probably appeared on the outward half.

Figure 60

After opening of the City Extension on 1 November 1865 it appears that the NLR operated a service between Dalston Junction and Fenchurch Street, until the opening of Poplar station on 1 August 1866. From that date Poplar became the NLR terminus and Fenchurch Street was served by a connecting shuttle service from and to Bow. These trains started to call at Shadwell on 1 October 1866, before that date a change at Stepney would have been required. Fares between Poplar and other NLR stations were the standard flat fares of single 6d first class and 4d second class, returns 9d and 6d. The running direction from Bow to Poplar appears to have been up, continuing that from Dalston Junction to Bow and the same as that from Bow to Fenchurch Street. Confirmation is offered by the only known Poplar ticket from this period, the red (down colour) half shown in Figure 61.

Withdrawal of the through Fenchurch Street service resulted in a number of passenger complaints, but the company resisted the pressure and maintained the shuttle service until 31 December 1868. They then withdrew entirely from Fenchurch Street and the connecting service from Bow was

Figure 61

taken over by the Great Eastern Railway. That company had leased the L&BR from 1 January 1866, and although the latter company retained nominal independence until the grouping it became for all practical purposes a part of the GER from the leasing date.

The earliest known ticket conforming to paragraph 3 of G.O.32 is a single to an HJR station, shown in Figure 62, white with a red stripe. It is of Type LOS1, untitled, and is thus a pre-1870 print despite the 1873 issue date. Note the instructions to change both at Bow (from the shuttle service) and at Dalston Junction. Contemporary return halves are shown in Figures 63 (white with a red stripe) and 64 (blue with a white stripe), the latter showing a very early occurrence of a specially printed child ticket. Again, these show the class at the top of the ticket.

Figure 62

Figure 63

Figure 64

Turning to tickets to and from L&B stations east of Stepney Junction these never, so far as is known, identified an individual L&BR station but simply referred to "Blackwall Railway". All known tickets for such bookings are modified from the standard local Types by having the class at the top of the ticket and showing the fare, and, in the case of singles by having the serial number at each end of the ticket. Returns of modified Type LOR1 are recorded for the outward journey Blackwall Railway to Bow on white/yellow card with a single broad central transverse brown stripe and for the outward journey Bow to Blackwall Railway on yellow/white card with a similar stripe, following G.O.32. The stripes are repeated on the backs of the tickets.

The transverse stripe, however, was very short-lived, by mid-1866 its direction had been changed; a yellow single dated 12 March 1867 with a brown longitudinal stripe is shown in Figure 65, and Figure 66 shows a return half dated 30 July 1866 having the same colours, the remaining part of the outward half shows that the base colour was white. The back is white, also with a brown longitudinal stripe.

Figure 65

Figure 66

It is not known if these tickets to the east of Stepney survived withdrawal of the NLR Bow - Fenchurch Street service, but they would certainly not have survived the next Bow line development. This was the building of a curve from south of Poplar (NLR) to the L&BR west of their Poplar station; through running from Poplar (NLR) to Blackwall was thus enabled and from 1 September 1870 Blackwall became the eastern terminus of the NLR.

Through NLR tickets to Stepney, Shadwell and Fenchurch Street continued to be available, but journeys to these stations were thereafter considered to be foreign bookings and these later tickets will be dealt with in Chapter Ten.

LOCAL TICKETS BEYOND BOW 1870-1890

Blackwall was treated as a local station, it may have been allocated a code letter for use on Short Journey tickets to Poplar. Logically, the running direction from Poplar to Blackwall would have been up, as a simple continuation of the existing system. Tickets issued at Blackwall should therefore have been in the down colours of white, red and green. However, Borley states (with no authority given) that "*NL tickets were issued there, but very few survived and it would appear that these were at first of the usual up line colours, but later the down line colours were adopted*". Initial practice, it is suggested, was thus the opposite of what would have been expected.

Borley is right on scarcity, but how do the existing specimens support his statement on colour? Discounting the early yellow ticket of Figure 15 (via Stepney and the L&BR) the known ordinary singles, two of which are shown in Figures 67 and 68,

Figure 67

Figure 68

are listed below:

Blackwall - Victoria Park	Type LOS3	23 MY 74	2nd class Blue
Blackwall - Bow	Type LOS5	09 MR 80	1stclass Yellow
Blackwall - Poplar	Type LOS6	14 AU 80	1st class Yellow
Blackwall - Dalston Jct	Type LOS6	30 AP 81	2nd class Blue
Blackwall - Poplar	Type LOS6	15 JY 80	3rd class Buff
Shoreditch - Blackwall	Type LOS3	17 OC 70	1st class White
Camden Rd - Blackwall	Type LOS3	29 OC ?	2nd class Red
Gospel Oak - Blackwall	Type LOS3	27 OC ?	2nd class Red

One ordinary return half is also known, from Blackwall to Broad Street, on yellow card with the remaining vestige of the outward half white.

All these tickets confirm reversal of the expected colours during the 1870s and early 1880s, tickets from Blackwall were in the up colours, those to it in the down colours. No bi-directional stripe appears on the single to Dalston Junction, the single from Shoreditch or the Broad Street return half.

Why did this reversal occur? One logical explanation could be that it was so agreed with the GER during negotiations for the use of Blackwall station. The GER also used directional colouring for their tickets, Blackwall was the terminus of the L&B line and would thus only collect down tickets. The GER down colours for ordinary singles were white, red and green, the same as the NLR up colours so the NLR effected the change to simplify checking at Blackwall.

The second part of Borley's contention is that later on the down line colours were adopted for Blackwall issues, i.e. tickets from Blackwall became white, red and green. No single tickets are known that support this premise, but one solitary return half shows that this may have been the case, the red Type LOR5t issue shown in Figure 69 - the outward half will have been blue.

Figure 69

If there was a change, however, it may have applied to return tickets only and here again GER practice could be relevant. In 1870 GER ordinary returns were printed on card of a single colour, those for an up outward and down return journey were white, red and green for the three classes (as for down singles), those for a down outward and up return journey were yellow, blue and buff (as for up singles). Uniquely, it is thought, amongst the English railway companies the GER printed the outward half on the left and the return half on the right. For GER tickets, therefore, the Blackwall collectors will have retained yellow, blue and buff left hand (outward) halves and white, red and green right hand (return) halves.

Within the NLR system of directional colouring it would not have been possible to match the GER collection, as outward and return halves to Blackwall would all have been of the same colour; the logic could thus have been to make halves to Blackwall the same colour as singles to Blackwall. Colours of return tickets issued to Blackwall would then have been yellow/white, blue/red and buff/green, while those issued at Blackwall would have been white/yellow, red/blue and green/buff, in each case reversing the expected colours. All NLR halves retained at Blackwall would have been white, red and green, the left hand (return) halves being of opposite colours to GER left hand halves and the right hand (outward) halves being of the same colours as GER right hand halves.

By 1877 the GER had changed to bi-coloured ordinary return tickets, up halves being white, red and green and down halves being yellow, blue and buff; somewhat perversely these were the opposite colours to those used for ordinary singles! The outward half continued to be on the left. All GER halves collected at Blackwall will then have been yellow, blue and buff, the same effect could only be obtained for NLR issues by reversing the earlier colours so that tickets issued to Blackwall became white/yellow, red/blue and green/buff with those issued at Blackwall becoming yellow/white, blue/red and buff/green, adoption of the normal NLR up and down colour pattern.

The colours of GER singles did not change, and thus no change would have been needed for NLR singles. Although there is an appealing logic to this theory of an interface with the GER, and although it fits known tickets and is consistent with Borley if his colour change statement was based on ordinary returns, it must be emphasised that it is purely speculative.

Speculation must also surround Poplar tickets during the period that Blackwall was served by the NLR. Before Blackwall opened, Poplar was at the end of an up line extension from Bow and tickets to it should have been yellow, blue and buff, it will be recalled that the ticket of Figure 61 offers some confirmation of this. Only one ticket is known to support continuation of standard colours after the opening of Blackwall, a green third single of Type LOS5 from Poplar to Camden Town shown in Figure 70. Other examples, however, e.g. the white single shown in Figure 71, contradict this to suggest that a little later Poplar was treated the same as

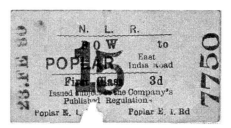

Figure 71

Blackwall, with the Bow - Poplar direction being treated as down:

Bow - Poplar	Type LOS5	23 FE 80	1st class White
Poplar - Bow	Type LOS5	23 JY 80	1st class Yellow
Poplar - Dalston Jct	Type LOS6	03 MY 87	3rd class Buff

There was a further complication; South Bromley, between Bow and Poplar, opened on 1 September 1884. No pre-1890 tickets to or from this station have been seen.

The NLR initially had their own staff at Blackwall, but in a cost-cutting exercise they were withdrawn on 1 January 1881 from which date the GER staff handled NLR matters. All was to no avail, the service did not succeed and was curtailed to Poplar on and from 1 July 1890.

LOCAL TICKETS BEYOND BOW 1890-1912

Withdrawal of NLR Blackwall services seems to have prompted another twist in the ticket colour scheme, as it is probably from this date that many tickets to and from Poplar were given distinctive colours, as follows:-

From Poplar to stations South Bromley to Hackney inclusive (up to South Bromley then down) and to Poplar from City Extension stations including Dalston Junction (down/up to South Bromley then down):

	Single	Return	Longitudinal Marking
First class	White	Yellow/white	Blue stripe
Second class	Red	Blue/white/red	Three red stripes
Third class	Green		Buff stripe
Third class		Buff/green	Orange stripe

From Poplar to City Extension stations including Dalston Junction (up to South Bromley then down/up) and to Poplar from stations Hackney to South Bromley inclusive (up to South Bromley then down):

	Single	Return	Longitudinal Marking
First class	Yellow		Green stripe*
First class		White/yellow	Blue stripe
Second class	Blue	Red/white/blue	Three red stripes
Third class	Buff		Green stripe
Third class		Green/buff	Orange stripe

* The result of blue on yellow.

The theory has been proposed that these special colours were used to reflect the change of running direction beyond Bow, which simply continued as it had been during the time that Blackwall was open, subject to the possibility that South Bromley became the changeover point after it opened in 1884.

A more attractive explanation is that the closure of Blackwall enabled the anomalous running beyond Bow (or South Bromley) to be abolished, the full length of the line from Dalston East Junction to Poplar then becoming up. From the closing paragraphs of the previous section it will be realised that this abolition would have constituted the second reversal

Figure 70

of direction for Poplar, and to avoid the doubt that a simple reversion to the original colours may have caused the special colours were adopted.

The base colours underlying the special colour scheme would seem to support this. Taking first the non-City Extension tickets, those from Poplar have down base colours (for a wholly down journey) and those to Poplar have up base colours (for a wholly up journey). It seems to have become an over-riding priority that any ticket involving a City Extension station would have a base colour governed by the direction of travel on the Extension, thus down/up tickets from Extension stations to Poplar have down base colours, and down/up tickets from Poplar to Extension stations have up base colours. Specially coloured Poplar tickets are known in types LOS7, LOS8, LOR7, LOR8 and LOR9; examples are shown in Plate 4, non-matching halves are shown for some of the returns.

For journeys involving stations west of Dalston Junction, Poplar was treated the same as other Bow line stations and plain coloured cards with no special markings were used. Thus, such westbound tickets from Poplar were white, red and green and eastbound tickets to Poplar were yellow, blue and buff. Note that "Poplar" always appeared as the issuing station but as a destination it was always shown as "Poplar East India Road" to distinguish it from the GER Poplar station.

No special treatment was given to South Bromley, post-1890 ticket practice to and from there was the same as for any other one of the stations from Hackney to Bow.

ఌఓ

Chapter Seven

LOCAL TICKETS - ROUTING NOTICES

Paragraph 6 of G.O.32 stated that, unless specified, tickets were only available for trains travelling direct to the destination station. The "Change at South Acton" notice on the ticket of Figure 55 reflects this, as does the "Change at Dalston Junction" of the Figure 21 ticket and some of the tickets shown in Figures 61 to 70. Following the closure of Kingsland there was no through passenger working between the Main Line and the Bow Line (except for some long-distance excursion traffic) and all tickets between Main Line, including N&SWJR, stations and Bow Line stations carried the change notice, in either upper or lower case, other examples are shown in Figures 72 (buff) and 73 (green/buff).

Figure 72

Figure 73

The ticket of Figure 21, for a journey to Bow, also carries the notice "Not available beyond", that of Figure 63 states "Not available at Bow, or Broad St". Such notices have only been seen on early prints and were perhaps only in use during the period of through running to Fenchurch Street, which ceased with the opening of Poplar station on 1 August 1866.

From the opening of the City Extension the HJR and N&SWJR were served by trains running fast between Broad Street and Camden Town, stopping only at Dalston Junction and Shoreditch, the latter being changed to Islington from 1 February 1868. Passengers from other City Extension and Main Line stations wishing to travel to HJR or N&SWJR stations were therefore required to change and tickets carried a notice accordingly. Originally the notice was "Change at Camden Town", later "Via Camden Town", Figures 74 and 75 (both buff). N&SWJR tickets for the reverse journeys carried the same notice. For some years passengers from Chalk Farm to the N&SWJR and vice versa had the facility of travelling either via Camden Town and changing, or via trains running over the L&NWR through Loudoun Road to Willesden and changing, and the alternative routing was shown as on the pink ticket of Figure 76.

Figure 74

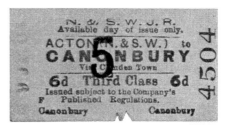

Figure 75

Figure 76

LOCAL TICKETS - BOOKING OFFICES

Booking office indications appear only to have been used at Bow, Hackney, Victoria Park and Caledonian Road & Barnsbury (No 1 and No 2 in each case) and at Dalston Junction, from where tickets marked (E.O.) have been seen.

From 4 April 1892 Bow was linked to the Great Eastern Railway's Bow Road station by a covered footway. Bow No 2 office adjoined the footway, it appears to have come into use shortly after the link as an LS&TC Minute dated 14 May records that Mr Gregar was to supply a new ticket case for the interchange station at Bow for the sum of £12-10-0. Bow No 2 tickets showed the booking office number after the station

Figure 77

name (Figure 77, buff with green stripe), tickets from the main office simply showed "Bow".

Hackney No 2 office was mentioned in Chapter 5 as in use from 1 December 1885, and having station code 10A allocated to it. That code would only have appeared on return halves of tickets issued at the No 2 office, and it is more than likely that it was used to facilitate the sorting of the collected halves for audit purposes. The No 2 office was staffed by the GER and would have had a different accounting regime, a clear distinction was thus essential. A single from the No 2 office, blue with a red stripe, is shown in Figure 78; as with Bow, tickets from the main office simply showed the station name.

Figure 78

Victoria Park issues showed No 1 or No 2 after the station name (Figure 79, green), the main office faced onto Cadogan Square and the Park while the "Hackney Wick" (No 2) office was located in Riseholme Street. It opened on 1 February 1899, an LS&TC Minute of 1 March reports *"the supply of ticket cases for the new booking office at Victoria Park"*.

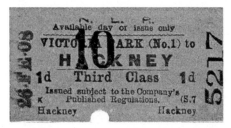

Figure 79

A Board Minute of 6 February 1893 notes acceptance of Mr Gregar's tender for six new ticket cases for the new booking office at Barnsbury at a cost of £75. The office, at the west end of the platforms, opened on 22 May 1893 on which date the

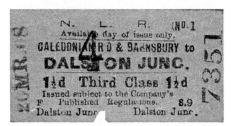

Figure 80

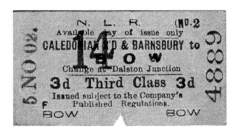

Figure 81

station was renamed Caledonian Road & Barnsbury. Probably due to the length of the station name the booking office indication No.1 or No.2 appeared prominently at the top of the ticket, Figures 80 and 81 (both buff).

The "E.O." office at Dalston Junction (Figure 82, buff) remains something of a mystery. Thought to be the 'East Office' it is believed to have been located in Roseberry Place and connected to the Broad Street end of the platforms by a covered footbridge.

Figure 82

LOCAL TICKETS - CHILD

As already stated, specially printed child tickets appear to have been little used, children usually being issued with the bisected half an adult ticket. In this connection the Regulation of Railways Act of 1889 caused the company some concern. That Act imposed a legal obligation to show the fare paid on the face of all ordinary, i.e. full fare tickets (and those in some other categories), and imposed a penalty of forty shillings for every ticket issued otherwise. The Act came into force on 1 July 1890, the company had shown the fare on local tickets as a matter of course from 1875 and to that degree complied with the requirement. For the avoidance of doubt, however, the Board approved a letter to the Board of Trade on 15 May 1890, requesting permission to continue the issue of half adult tickets to children in cases where bookings were limited, instead of providing separate children's tickets with consequent duplication of stock and of case accommodation. Obviously each bisected half would show the adult rather than the child fare, in possible contravention of the Act. Presumably the reply was favourable, as bisection continued.

It may be from this time, however, that specially printed child singles came into use. Only one local issue is known, the green ticket of Type LOS8 shown in Figure 83. Returns had

Figure 83

been used from an earlier date, they are known in untitled Type LOR2, showing "Child's Return" and "Child's Ticket" at the top of the return (Figure 84, red) and outward halves respectively, and in Types LOR4 to LOR9. Figure 85 shows a red/blue example of Type LOR7 and Figure 86 a white/yellow example of Type LOR8. All known returns are to Broad Street, from NLR stations west and east of Dalston Junction; colours of both singles and returns are the same as for the corresponding adult issues.

From the mid-1890s child tickets were supplied to the booking offices with a trapezoidal snip as in Figure 83 and 86 taken

Figure 84

Figure 85

Figure 86

from the bottom of the ticket, following the practice used by the L&NWR. It will be recalled that Waterlow's 1899 tender included the item *"Child's tickets with piece cut out 1/- per thousand extra"*.

LOCAL TICKETS - ODDITIES

Considering the complexities of the ticket system the degree of accuracy in supplying tickets of the right format appears to have been incredibly good and few oddities are found.

Figure 87 shows one of these, it is on the correct white card with a red stripe but the miniature repeats of the destination station expected on a Type LOS6 ticket are replaced by an audit snip containing repeats of the two stations at the centre of the foot of the ticket. This is standard foreign format (dealt with in Chapter Eight) rather than local format as should have been the case. A second class single from Shoreditch to Bow dated 11 Nov 1890, and a third class single from Poplar to Islington & Highbury dated 4 August 1890, both again in what should have been Type LOS6, are also known with this

Figure 87

presumed error. One return is also known, a third class issue from Dalston Junction to Camden Town in what should have been Type LOR6b.

Figure 88 shows a pink return half of Type LOR6t with the printcode, dated 14 September 1880. This should have had the fare printed to the right of the class. The initials RP may have been noted to the right of the conditions in Figure 76; although uncommon on local tickets these initials appear reasonably frequently on those for foreign journeys. It is virtually certain that the initials indicate a re-print, i.e. a batch of original stock has been withdrawn and replaced by new, amended tickets bearing the same serial numbers.

Figure 88

Finally in this Chapter, the return half shown in Figure 89 is a complete mystery. The left hand part is blue and the right hand white, with three longitudinal red stripes, the correct "Poplar" colours for the journey (see Plate 4), but a red transverse stripe has been added to the white section of the half and the initials WE have been added to the station code. The 3d fare is the full ordinary fare for the journey concerned.

Figure 89

Chapter Eight

THE FORMAT OF FOREIGN TICKETS 1865-1912

Before considering in detail tickets to destinations off the NLR it is necessary to trace the development of foreign, as opposed to local, prints. This Chapter deals with the format only, it does not deal with colours or routing notices, which will be discussed in later Chapters dealing with bookings to specific companies. As with local tickets, no attempt has been made to codify foreign prints prior to 1865; the correlation between local and foreign Types after that year is tabulated on the following page.

Waterlow-printed Types LOS1 and LOR1 served equally well both for local and for foreign bookings. The same almost certainly applied to Types LOS2, LOR2 and LOR3 (probably in version LOR3b only) but the advent of local Type LOS3 was probably accompanied by the introduction of distinct foreign tickets. Type LOS3 showed miniature repeats of the destination at each side of the foot of the ticket; some other companies used similar repeats and, like the NLR, vertically bisected tickets for issue to children. Others did not, preferring to remove a trapezoidal section (the "audit snip") from the centre of the lower edge of the ticket when the ticket was issued to a child. The audit snip had printed on it at least the name of the destination station, and booking clerks were required to gum the snips on to special sheets and return them to the audit office as evidence of the half fare they had collected for the child issue. It seems that the NLR, with through bookings to many different companies, did not wish to concern themselves with which companies used which system and so decided simply to use the audit snip system for all foreign bookings.

Thus, the first specific foreign singles have an audit snip, a green example of Type FOS1 is shown in Figure 90, the Type has been seen with issue dates from 2 July 1872 onwards. This Type continued in use down to 1880, unlike local tickets the fare does not seem to have been added to foreign prints in 1875. In 1880 foreign tickets, as with local issues, gained a

Figure 90

Figure 91

printcode to give Type FOS2, shown in Figure 91 (white). By February 1887 the name of the issuing station had been added to the audit snip to give Type FOS3 (Figure 92, buff).

Figure 92

By the time that the Regulation of Railways Act 1889 came into force on 1 July 1890 the fare had been added to foreign tickets to give Type FOS4 (Figure 93, green). When the fare was added to the left of the class on local tickets there was no corresponding change on foreign prints, as vertical bisection was not practised. Foreign single Type FOS5 showed the availability below the title (Figure 94, buff).

Figure 93

Figure 94

Local returns did not carry miniature repeats; foreign returns, as with singles, had audit snips. Initially these showed the destination station only, and there were three such Types. The first of these, FOR1 (Figure 95, blue/red), carried no station codes; Type FOR2 (illustrated by non-matching halves in Figure 96) had a station code on the return half, and was presumably introduced when the station code system was changed in November 1873. Type FOR3 was similar to FOR2, but with the printcode added, and is illustrated by non-matching halves in Figure 97.

Type FOR4 showed both stations in the audit snip, Figure 98 (buff/green). Type FOR5 (Figure 99, blue/red) became standard when the fare was shown on all foreign returns from July 1890, although it must be stated that the fare had appeared on earlier tickets for some bookings as will be dealt

Correlation between local and foreign Waterlow prints

Feature	Earliest Date Seen	Local Singles	Foreign Singles	Local Returns	Foreign Returns
Untitled	Jul 1866	LOS1 LOS1SJ	LOS1	LOR1	LOR1
Not transferable	Jan 1867	No change	No change	LOR2 LOR2SJ	LOR2
Title added	Feb 1870	LOS2 LOS2SJ	LOS2	LOR3b LOR3bSJ LOR3t LOR3tSJ	LOR3b
Miniature repeats (local)/audit snip (foreign)	Oct 1870	LOS3 LOS3SJ	FOS1*	No change	FOR1
Later station codes	Nov 1873	LOS4	No change	LOR4b LOR4t	FOR2*
Fare added	May 1875	LOS5	No change	LOR5b LOR5t	No change
Printcode	Feb 1880	LOS6	FOS2*	LOR6b LOR6t	FOR3*
Issuing station named in snip	Feb 1887	No change	FOS3*	No change	FOR4*
Fare to left	Apr 1888	LOS7	No change	LOR7	No change
Fare added	Jul 1890	No change	FOS4	No change	FOR5
Availability	May 1897	LOS8	FOS5	LOR8	FOR6
Later availability	Aug 1902	No change	No change	LOR9	FOR7
Multiple destinations	Jan 1906	LOS9	No change	LOR10	No change
Station codes omitted	Dec 1910	LOS10	No change	LOR11	No change

* Occasional tickets of this Type are known with a printed fare.

Figure 95

Figure 96

Figure 97

Figure 98

Figure 99

Figure 100

with in later Chapters. Unlike local tickets the fare was not moved to the left of the class on the return half. On Type FOR6 day of issue availability is shown on the return half, Type FOR7 (Figure 100, buff/green) shows the later two day availability.

The availability of foreign returns differed according to destination company and to distance, they are set out in General Order No 188; this was revised in October 1891, unfortunately in RAIL 529/110 the revision is pasted over the original so that neither date nor contents can be determined. Further revisions were dated August 1892, May 1898 and 28 July 1902 and the Order was eventually superseded by General Order No 389, in force from 30 June 1904. Availabilities will be dealt with in detail when discussing bookings to individual companies, but it is thought that for both singles and returns the availability was only shown as a matter of course on tickets to HJ line and other L&NWR destinations.

ಶೋಡಿ

Chapter Nine

THE HAMPSTEAD JUNCTION LINE 1872-1912

The HJR passed into L&NWR ownership on 15 July 1867, but this had no affect on operation or on ticket practice, and tickets printed by the NLR but titled Hampstead Junction Rly remained in use. All was to change from 1 July 1872 when the L&NWR took possession of the line. Heads of Agreement were submitted to the Boards of the NLR and L&NWR in June 1872, and included the following provisions:

"1) That the L&NWR shall pay the NLR for the Passenger Trains to be run by them over the Hampstead Junction Railway one shilling per train mile; such allowance to cover the cost of conveying in NL Trains the local and through passenger traffic of the L&NWR.

2) That the NLR shall pay the L&NWR for the Passenger Trains run by them over the NL Line ninepence per train mile; such allowance to cover the cost of conveying in NW Trains, the local and through traffic of the NL Company.

3) The Station Staff of the HJ Line to be found and performed by the L&NW Company, the NL Company performing similar duties with respect to the NL Line.

4/5) That at the request of the L&NW Company the NL Company shall run a service of Passenger Trains between Chalk Farm Station and Willesden Low Level Station, at such time as shall be mutually agreed, the LNW to pay the NL one shilling per train mile.

6) That in respect of all LNW passenger traffic conveyed over the N&SWJR, in NL trains, so long as the LNW do not run their own passenger trains, they shall pay to the NL Company twopence per train mile for the conveyance of such passenger traffic.

7) For traffic booked through between NL stations and stations north of Willesden, or on West London, West London Extension and Metropolitan District Railways the LNW to pay to the NLR out of their through fares, as the proportion due between the Camden Road Junction and Dalston, Shoreditch, and Broad Street stations, and for stations between Dalston and Camden Road, 4d per first class, 3d per second and third class passenger holding single tickets, and 6d per first class and 4d second class return tickets. The fares for east of Dalston to be the Camden fares plus the North London local fares from Camden Road, the NL to be credited its local fare out of these bookings."

Thus the L&NWR took over the HJ Line booking offices and commenced to issue standard L&NWR titled tickets. Immediately before the changeover Types LOS3 and LOR3t were in use. The latest issue dates seen on HJR titled tickets are 28 Sep 1872 and 26 Aug 1873, the earliest date seen on an L&NWR titled print is 14 Feb 1873, for a relatively little used 3rd Parly journey Hampstead Heath - Brompton Gloucester Road. These tie in nicely with a gradual re-stocking of the booking offices from July 1872 and disprove Borley's suggestion that this change did not occur until July 1874. Perhaps the work had been completed by then.

L&NWR titled tickets from HJR stations play no further part in this work, but as NLR trains between Broad Street and the N&SWJR continued to pass over the HJ Line, tickets from NLR and N&SWJR stations to that Line must be dealt with. These involved a mixture of local and foreign practice.

General Order No 115 stated that as from its date (September 1873) *"tickets issued from stations on the Hampstead Junction line will not at present be numbered"*, i.e. will not bear station codes. Codes were, however, allocated to those stations and NLR and N&SWJR tickets to them duly carried those codes. Initially these were standard local prints of Types LOS4 and LOR4t (Figure 101), NLR titled in the down colours of white, red and green for singles, yellow/white, blue/red and buff/green for returns, and N&SWJ titled in the up colours of yellow, blue and buff for singles, white/yellow, red/blue and green/buff for returns. Similar groups of tickets then appeared, from May 1875 in Types LOS5 (Figure 102) and LOR5t showing the fare to the right of the class and from 1880 in Types LOS6 (Figure 103) and LOR6t with the printcode added.

Figure 101

Figure 102

Figure 103

During the currency of Types LOS6 and LOR6t a change was made to third class tickets, to show the class as "Third Class (Parly)" (Figure 104), the colours remaining the same. The earliest issue date known for such tickets is July 1884. Presumably the change was at the request of the L&NWR who, until at least mid-1897, retained some differential Third Class and Parliamentary fares, albeit for single journeys only from about 1890.

Type LOR6t was short-lived and replaced by LOR6b. Types LOS7 and LOR7 with the fare to the left of the class appeared

Figure 104

Figure 108

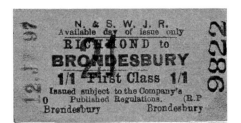

Figure 105

Figure 109

from 1888. These were followed from May 1897 by Types LOS8 (Figure 105) and LOR8, showing the availability. At some time during the 1890s, while Types LOS7 and LOR7 were current the title "N. & S. W. JUNC." was changed to appear as "N. & S.W.J.R." (compare Figures 102 and 105).

By March 1900 the "Parly" designation had been dropped, possibly at the same time it was realised that tickets to HJ Line stations were not local at all, they were purely foreign and should be treated as such. The format for single tickets then changed to FOS5hj (Figure 106), with an audit snip at the centre of the lower edge of the ticket, but with one important difference from the standard foreign Type FOS5 in that the fare was repeated to the left of the class. Similar changes were made to return tickets to give Type FOR6hj (Figure 107) and then FOR7hj (Figure 108), each modified from the standard foreign Type FOR6 or FOR7 by showing the

later ones omitted this. All had the audit snip, but because of the space restrictions caused by this the conditions clause was relegated to the back of the ticket in form A1. Some alternative destination returns were also used, illustrated by the non-matching halves of Figure 110, with the conditions on the back in form B1.

Figure 110

Through tickets from Bow Line to HJ Line stations carried the notice "Change at Dalston Junction" (Figure 111), alternative destination prints and some other singles carried conditions A1 on the back, returns had conditions B1. Tickets from City Extension and Main Line stations other than Broad Street,

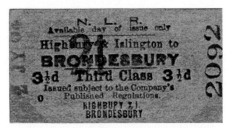

Figure 106

Figure 107

fare to the left, not the right, of the class on the return half. As with purely local NLR tickets there were some later alternative destination issues to HJ Line stations, the group of destinations sometimes also including Loudoun Road or Kilburn (Maida Vale) and even stations on the West London Railway (Figure 109). Earlier issues included a station code,

Figure 111

Figure 112

Dalston Jct and Highbury & Islington carried the "Change at Camden Town" notice (Figure 112), later changed to "Via Camden Town".

One specially printed child return to the HJ Line is known, in Type FOR7hj, shown in Figure 113.

Figure 113

❧❦

Chapter Ten

FOREIGN BOOKINGS

The NLR, HJR and N&SWJR at their fullest extent formed a semi-circle around the north of London, so giving wide scope for foreign tickets. Bookings were offered to certain stations of all the main line companies serving London, except for the Great Central and the South Eastern Railways, as well as to the Metropolitan District Railway. This chapter will first complete the story of the Fenchurch Street line, tickets to other foreign stations down to 1912 will then be dealt with in alphabetical order of destination company.

BOW - FENCHURCH STREET 1870-1912

It has already been mentioned that when Poplar opened on 1 August 1866 through NLR running beyond Bow to Fenchurch Street ceased and a shuttle service commenced to operate between those stations. From close of business on 31 December 1868 the NLR withdrew from Fenchurch Street, presumably supply of NLR tickets to that and the other L&BR stations would then have stopped. From the following day the shuttle service was taken over by the Great Eastern Railway, continuing to call at Stepney and Shadwell and, from its opening on 11 September 1871, Burdett Road. Despite these events through bookings from NLR stations continued to be offered, the October 1870 tables show fares to Fenchurch Street from Kew Bridge, Hammersmith and Acton and all HJ Line and NLR stations except Broad Street, Poplar and Blackwall; fares to Stepney from all that group of stations except Shoreditch; and fares to Shadwell from all that group except Shoreditch, Hammersmith and stations from Acton to Finchley Road inclusive.

Figure 114 shows a ticket for one such booking, of foreign Type FOS1 with an audit snip showing the destination only. Surprisingly, it does not carry the legend "Change at Bow", although it must have been via the shuttle service.

Figure 114

By late 1876 the GER was complaining that the shuttle service was unremunerative and threatening to withdraw it. The NLR countered by promising to run a half-hourly service if this happened, and the threat was not carried out. Tickets for the shuttle service were issued from the NLR office at Bow, it was thus logical for them to be supplied by Waterlow but they were distinguished by carrying the title of the operating company (Figures 115 and 116). These examples are buff, the GER colour for up tickets. Note the rare appearance on a foreign single of a printed fare on Figure 115; apart from this the ticket is in the format of Type FOS2, that of Figure 116 is of Type FOS3.

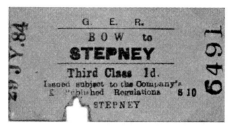

Figure 115

Figure 116

The demise of the shuttle service finally came on 4 April 1892, when the GER decided that it would be more economical to withdraw it, re-site their existing Bow Road station and provide a covered footway between Bow and Bow Road so that passengers could easily transfer between the two stations to change trains. Again, through bookings from some NLR and N&SWJR stations survived the change, an example of Type FOR5 is shown in Figure 117. This reflects the existence of the footway by stating "Change at Bow Road", the notice on the outward half will have been "Change at Bow". The footway closed in 1917.

Figure 117

Colours for these tickets must now be considered. Paragraph 3 of G.O.32 (quoted in Chapter 6) applied to all tickets between NLR (and N&SWJR) stations and Stepney, Shadwell and Fenchurch Street. Up colours, for singles and outward halves towards Fenchurch Street were first class yellow with a transverse red stripe and second class blue with a transverse white stripe; the tickets of Figures 64 and 114 fit this pattern. Down colours, only applicable to return halves, were first class white with a red stripe and second class red with a white stripe, as in Figure 117. G.O.32 dealt with third class tickets in the context of early Parliamentary bookings only and gave no special colours for third class tickets for these journeys to and from the three GE stations. When these were introduced, therefore, it is not surprising that plain card was used; indeed this continued to be the case, examples in the expected up colour of buff are known and the down colour (applicable to return halves only) will have been green.

G.O.32 specified that the only City Extension station at which these bookings could be made was Dalston Junction. The normal base colours for all tickets for journeys from the City Extension were the down colours of white, red and green. The earliest tickets from Dalston Junction to these GE stations were thus anomalous in using the up base colours of yellow, blue and buff. Probably by the turn of the century, however, (and possibly from the introduction of special colours for Poplar) this anomaly had been addressed and tickets from Dalston to the GE stations were thereafter in down base colours. Singles and outward halves of returns were thus first class white with a red stripe, second class red with a white stripe and third class green. Return halves were yellow with a red stripe, blue with a white stripe and buff. Single tickets of this later period are illustrated in Plate 5.

GREAT EASTERN RAILWAY

The Victoria Park branch of the Eastern Counties Railway was opened on 15 August 1854, but very little use was made of the line until 16 October 1854 when an NLR passenger service commenced. Through Hampstead Road - Stratford Bridge coaches were provided, detached from the main NLR trains at Victoria Park Junction (no station was then provided) and calling at the Low Level platforms at Stratford; in addition there were some summer Sunday through trains. Victoria Park station was opened for regular traffic on 14 June 1856, it had opened specially on 29 May 1856 in connection with the Peace Celebrations held in the Park to mark the end of the Crimean War. The through carriages, but not the through Sunday trains, ceased at the end of December 1859 so that from 1 January 1860 passengers to the ECR usually had to change at Victoria Park.

The ECR amalgamated with other companies on 7 August 1862 to form the Great Eastern Railway. On 1 March 1866 the original Victoria Park was replaced by a new station, from 1 September that year the NLR ceased to work passenger trains to Stratford Bridge, and from 1 November the GER provided a local service between Victoria Park and Stratford Bridge. This was again taken over by the NLR from 1 November 1867 and thereafter the GER and NLR worked the service in alternate years until 31 October 1874 when the last NLR train ran. Stratford Bridge was renamed Stratford Market on 1 November 1880 and replaced by a new station in 1892. From 1 October 1895 the GER trains were extended to Canning Town and at various periods thereafter they worked through to North Woolwich. All known tickets to GER stations from Victoria Park were printed by the GER and carried their title, they are thus outside the scope of this work.

The January 1856 timetables show fares from stations Hampstead Road to Hackney inclusive as follows:

| | Single | | Return | |
	First	Second	First	Second
Stratford or Stratford Bridge	6d	4d	9d	6d
Barking Rd, Custom House (Victoria Dock), North Woolwich or Woolwich*	8d	6d	1/4	1/-

* Designated as Woolwich Roff's Wharf, including boat.

One odd feature of GER bookings is tickets to Woolwich Town, never a recognised station name. These must have been for use to South Woolwich via the GER ferry service, started by the ECR in the late 1840s. It is, however, difficult to reconcile this with the above table and with the fare tables of October

1870, which are confusing in referring to Woolwich (North) and Woolwich (South) at one fare and to Woolwich and Woolwich Town at a different fare, albeit for different issuing stations.

The October 1870 tables give fares for through bookings to all stations Stratford - Loughton and Stratford - North Woolwich (both inclusive) from Victoria Park and all NLR stations west thereof except Shoreditch and Broad Street, but not from HJ Line or N&SWJR stations. In later years some through tickets were issued at N&SWJR stations, and the list of GER destinations was expanded.

Tickets routed via Victoria Park will have existed in Types FOS1 to FOS4 and FOR1 to FOR5 and the expected colours would be the up colours of yellow, blue and buff for singles, white/yellow, red/blue and green/buff for returns. The half shown in Figure 118, with a red upper section and a blue lower section, indicates early use of a special colour scheme for at least some destinations, but (ignoring journeys from the City Extension) standard up colours were in use by the early 1880s as shown in Figures 119 (white, the outward half was yellow), 120 (blue) and 121 (buff).

Figure 118

Figure 119

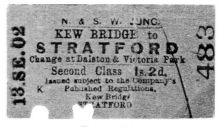

Figure 120

Figure 121

Figure 122

On 4 April 1892 the covered footway from Bow (NLR) to the GER station at Bow Road opened and tickets to the GER were made available via Victoria Park or Bow, Figure 122 (buff). These were in Types FOS4 and FOR5 and, from N&SWJR, Main Line and Bow Line stations west of Victoria Park, were in standard up colours. Those from Poplar and possibly South Bromley were in down colours. No colour suggestion is made for tickets from Old Ford lying, as it did, between Victoria Park and Bow.

There was yet a third interchange point to the GER on the Bow line, at Hackney where a covered footway to Hackney Downs (GER) was opened on 1 December 1885. Tickets to GER stations from NLR Main Line stations (changing at Dalston) were in up colours, those from stations east of Hackney in the down colours. Singles and outward halves of returns stated "Change at Hackney", Figure 123 (green), return halves stated "Change at Hackney Downs", Figure 124 (red).

Figure 123

Figure 124

No early tickets from City Extension stations have been seen, the later prints that are known (all from Dalston Junction) followed the rule that the base colour on the Extension took priority and were thus in the down colours irrespective of route.

Even this does not conclude the subject of the GER, there was also the possibility of travel to GE stations via the Tottenham & Hampstead Junction Rly, which will be considered in a later section.

Return availabilities to GER stations were day of issue and from Saturday to Monday in October 1891, August 1892 and May 1898; from July 1902 two days or Saturday to Monday for distances not exceeding 12 miles, otherwise eight days; and from June 1904 two days or Saturday to Monday for distances not exceeding 12 miles and six months for greater distances. No ticket has been seen with the availability printed thereon.

GREAT NORTHERN RAILWAY

A line from east-facing Canonbury Junction, between Canonbury and Highbury & Islington, to Finsbury Park was opened for passenger traffic on 18 January 1875. The aim was to relieve congestion on the GNR lines into Kings Cross and the initial thought was that the services would be operated by the GNR. However, the L&NWR objected to Broad Street being used by GNR trains, and services were therefore operated by NLR trains running between Broad Street and Barnet (renamed New Barnet 1 May 1884), Broad Street and

High Barnet, and from 1 February 1875 Broad Street and Enfield. Three classes were provided, sixteen NLR second class carriages having been converted into third class for the service in late 1874. From 1 August 1877 one train per day was extended beyond Barnet to work on to Hatfield, this was restricted to Potters Bar from December 1878, although there was still some sporadic working to Hatfield until May 1885. When the Enfield Loop opened on 4 April 1910 the limit of NLR operation was extended to Cuffley, being restricted to Gordon Hill from 1 May 1918. The company also ran trains to Alexandra Palace from its opening on 24 May 1873 and from its re-opening on 3 May 1875 following the disastrous fire of 9 June 1873.

According to Borley, Broad Street, Dalston Junction, Hackney, Bow and Poplar all had long distance tickets to a number of GNR and NER stations, supplied by the GNR. Examples are known from Broad Street and Dalston in standard GNR format and titled with the initials of that company. Most were withdrawn in 1916 from when few long distance trains called at Finsbury Park. Tickets for these bookings were then supplied by the NLR, but these would have been printed by the L&NWR and are dealt with in a later Chapter.

Tickets for suburban bookings were Waterlow printed and NLR titled from the outset. They are known in Types FOS1 to FOS4 and FOR2 to FOR5. Those from Canonbury, and early prints from City Extension stations (see Figure 90) carried no routing notice, early prints from the Bow Line showed "Change at Dalston Junc". Later tickets from stations east of Canonbury showed "via Canonbury" (Figure 125, white), with later tickets from the Bow line also showing "Change at Dalston". All of these (including Poplar issues) were, as would be expected, in the down colours. Tickets from NLR stations west of Canonbury carried the notice "Change at Canonbury" (Figure 126, buff) and were in up colours; tickets from N&SWJR stations were also in up colours, but carried the notice "Change at Dalston. Via Canonbury" (Figure 127). This reflected the fast running of the through N&SWJR line trains from Camden Town, calling only at Highbury &

Figure 125

Figure 126

Islington and at Dalston Junction.

Other routing notices are also found. As stated, Highbury & Islington was a stopping place for the fast trains from the N&SWJR and the ticket of Figure 128 thus gives the passenger the choice of a fast train changing at Dalston or of a slow train changing at Canonbury. This arrangement may have continued in later years. The ticket is in down colours of

Figure 127

Figure 128

blue/red, unexpected for a ticket from west of Canonbury. Whether this is an error or reflected earlier practice is not known. Some through tickets indicated a change of train at Finchley (Figure 129, green).

Figure 129

Specially printed child tickets to Finsbury Park are known, second class single and third class return (Figure 130, green) from Canonbury and third class single from Broad Street (Figure 131, green) and Mildmay Park, there may of course have been others. On earlier singles "CHILD'S TICKET" is shown above the class, these words are below the class on later prints.

Returns to GNR stations south of New Barnet, High Barnet, Edgware and Enfield inclusive were available for two days or from Saturday to Monday in October 1891 and August 1892, those north of New Barnet and not exceeding 50 miles for seven days, exceeding 50 miles one month; in May 1898 these availabilities became two days, eight days and one month respectively; from July 1902 availability to all stations south of Hadley Wood was two days or from Saturday to Monday, to Hadley Wood and not exceeding 50 miles eight days, over 50 miles one month; and from June 1904 not exceeding 12 miles two days or from Saturday to Monday, above 12 miles six months. No ticket has been seen with the availability printed thereon.

GREAT WESTERN RAILWAY

The GWR ran trains between Willesden Junction (High Level) and Southall from 2 January 1888. Through bookings were available from all NLR stations to stations between Windsor and Acton inclusive, an LS&TC Minute of 1 February 1888 authorised purchase of new ticket cases consequent on introduction of the new bookings. On 11 April 1888 that Committee recorded the issue of 239 cheap excursion tickets to GWR riverside stations at Easter. From 1 October 1904 ordinary trains were replaced by steam rail motors working through to Willesden from the Greenford Loop or in some cases to and from Southall. The service was withdrawn from 11 March 1912.

Tickets in Types FOS3 and FOR4 are theoretically possible but the only ones known are in the later types FOS4 and FOR5, showing a printed fare. Tickets to Acton GWR were in distinctive colours, presumably to distinguish them from issues to Acton N&SWJR, singles being white with a longitudinal red stripe, red with a longitudinal blue stripe and green with a longitudinal red stripe for the three classes. These are illustrated in Plate 2. Only one return is known, a third class outward half which is green with a transverse blue stripe (Figure 132). For stations beyond Acton tickets were in the ordinary down colours of white, red and green (Figure 133) for singles; yellow/white, blue/red and buff/green for returns. The routing from east of Dalston was given as "Change at Dalston Junction. Via Willesden & Acton G.W.R.". For stations from Broad Street to Camden Town it was "Via Willesden & Acton G.W.R". From Chalk Farm two routes were available and the notice was "Via Loudoun Road or

Figure 130

Figure 131

Figure 132

Figure 133

Camden Town Willesden & Acton GWR" (Figure 134). Tickets to Acton GWR obviously omitted that station from the routing notice.

Figure 134

From October 1904 at least some tickets made reference to the rail motor car (Figure 135). Some stations stocked blank cards specifically for bookings to the GWR, Figure 136 (green).

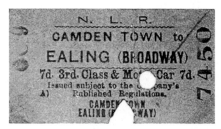

Figure 135

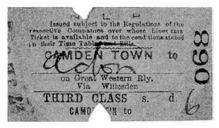

Figure 136

Return availabilities to GWR stations in October 1891 and August 1892 were two days where the single fare did not exceed 1/-, otherwise seven days; in May 1898 the seven day availability was extended to eight; from July 1902 availability was two days or from Saturday to Monday for distances not exceeding 12 miles, otherwise eight days; and from June 1904 it was two days or from Saturday to Monday for distances not exceeding 12 miles and six months for greater distances. Somewhat surprisingly a single is known of Type FOS5, showing the availability (Figure 137).

Figure 137

LONDON & NORTH WESTERN RAILWAY

It has already been stated that from 1 August 1853 NLR trains reached the N&SWJR via the L&NWR between Hampstead Road (later renamed Chalk Farm) and Willesden.

These trains began to call at Kilburn (L&NWR) on 1 June 1855, the January 1856 timetable gives single fares between Kilburn and any NLR or L&BR station as 8d first class and 6d second class, returns 1/- and 9d respectively. From Kilburn to Kew or Acton they were 1/3d first class and 1/- second class, returns 1/9d and 1/4d respectively. The yellow/white return ticket shown in Figure 138 almost certainly dates from this time. It is in two-coupon format rather than the single coupon format then used for local tickets (c/f Figures 3 to 8) It presumably differed because Kilburn was not an NLR station, the L&NWR staff at that station were used to collecting tickets at the end, rather than at the start, of the journey and the standard L&NWR return format was two-coupon.

Figure 138

Running by the NLR over the L&NWR ceased when the HJR opened on 2 January 1860. However, through bookings from NLR stations to Kilburn continued to be offered, passengers then changing at Hampstead Road. Fares to Euston were also quoted from an early date, again changing at Hampstead Road, the blue half shown in Figure 139 is a pre-1865 print. The original Willesden station closed on 1 September 1866,

Figure 139

being replaced by a new Willesden Junction station with Low Level platforms serving the L&NWR main line and High Level platforms serving the HJR and the Kew line. From that date some L&NWR trains between Broad Street and the north used a new curve from the south end of the Low Level platforms to the HJR; there was also some L&NWR working to Broad Street via Chalk Farm. Among the points agreed between the L&NWR and the NLR in 1866 were that:

"1. The NLR would provide the staff for the High Level station.

2. Local fares between Willesden Junction and NL stations be the same as then charged to and from Acton N&SWJ.

3. Holders of LNW Euston return tickets using any of the stations on the HJR or NLR will have to pay the local fare.

4. The LNW would pay out of their through fares to the NLR, as the proportion due between Camden Road Junction and any station from Camden Road to Broad Street 4d per First Class, 3d per Second and Third Class passenger holding single tickets, and 6d First Class and 4d second class Return Tickets.

5. Through booked passengers to be carried by the LNW between Camden Road Junction and Dalston, and by the NLR to and from Willesden and Stations east thereof, without charging or receiving working expenses in either case.

6. The LNW will be allowed for working expenses of traffic booked by their trains one third of the amount payable to the NLR on such traffic in respect of the line between Camden Road Junction or Broad Street and intermediate stations.

7. Through tickets with stations north of Willesden will be available by any of the trains running over the NL and HJ Rys; and NL passengers to be permitted to travel between Camden, Dalston, Shoreditch and Broad Street by LNW trains.

8. The fares for stations east of Dalston to be the Euston fares, plus the NL local fares from Camden Road, the NL to be credited its local fare out of these bookings."

On 2 January 1868 it was agreed that the L&NWR through train from Broad Street to Watford be reserved for L&NWR passengers only and that the 4.10, 4.40, 5.10 and 5.40 p.m. Broad Street to Kensington trains be reserved for passengers to the HJR, Kensington and the L&NWR main line.

Long distance through bookings to L&NWR stations were introduced in 1857. A Board Minute dated 29 September recorded that the L&NWR have agreed for the NLR to book passengers from Fenchurch Street and NLR stations for the four trains from Euston to Manchester, changing at Camden. The list of destinations expanded rapidly. At a meeting between the NLR and L&NWR on 14 July 1868 a list of through booking stations was submitted; on behalf of the NLR Mr Mansel explained *"the great difficulty of carrying out the system of blank cards hitherto adopted in most cases in consequence of the time necessarily occupied by clerks not conversant with LNW bills in ascertaining fares and train arrangements and afterwards filling up the tickets".* It was agreed that through booking to and from the NLR should be confined to a list of 39 stations and that passengers for all other L&NWR stations should only be booked locally to Willesden. Tickets and any necessary ticket cases were to be supplied by the L&NWR audit office for all these bookings and the blank card tickets were to be called in. The L&NWR were part owners of Broad Street and by 2 November 1869 had its own booking office, tickets issued there for L&NWR trains then carried that company's title. All these lie outside the scope of this work.

From 2 June 1879 some of the NLR Broad Street - Chalk Farm local trains were extended to Willesden (Low Level), calling at Kilburn and at the new stations opened that day at Loudoun Road and Queen's Park. Kilburn was renamed Kilburn & Maida Vale from 1 June 1879 but shown as Kilburn (Maida Vale) on NLR tickets, Loudoun Road was shown with the suffix (For Swiss Cottage) on NLR tickets. NLR titled tickets to these stations, and to Euston, were then issued at Main Line, City Extension and Bow Line stations. Apart from one early print of Type FOS1 (Figure 140), all these carry the routing "Via Chalk Farm", together with "Change at Dalston" if from the Bow Line. As expected, they are in the down colours of white, red and green for singles; yellow/white, blue/red and buff/green for returns. They are known in Types FOS1 to FOS5, also FOR2 to FOR7.

Figure 140

Initially the designation "Third Class" was used, but as with issues to HJ Line stations this had been changed to "Third Class (Parly)" by 1884. Later returns of Type FOR4 abbreviated this to "3rd Parly", and there could have been a reversion to "Third Class" for all such tickets in about March 1900 although no examples have been seen.

Through singles to Euston via Willesden are also known from N&SWJR stations, in Types FOS4 (Figure 141) and FOS5 and in the expected up colours of yellow, blue and buff. It is assumed that there were corresponding returns. There may also have been tickets to the other three L&NWR stations between Willesden and Euston.

Figure 141

Both single and return tickets to the L&NWR showed the availability from about 1897 (Types FOS5 - Figure 142, FOR6 and FOR7). In October 1891, August 1892 and May 1898 returns to stations Euston to Willesden were available for day of issue only and from Saturday to Monday, amended by G.O.188 dated 28 July 1902 to two days or from Saturday to Monday.

Figure 142

LONDON & SOUTH WESTERN RAILWAY

Three through trains between Hampstead Road and Windsor were put on from 1 June 1854, being hauled from Kew (the original station) to Windsor via Brentford by L&SWR locos. Fares were not to be less than those from Waterloo plus 3d first and 2d second and third class; the service lasted only until the end of October, when through running beyond Kew ceased. From 20 May 1858 NLR carriages began running to Richmond and Twickenham by reversing twice, at Kew and at Barnes, while L&SWR carriages ran to Hampstead Road in approximately alternate trains. It appears that when the HJR opened on 2 January 1860 these services were diverted from Willesden over that line to terminate at Camden Road. From 1 February 1860 there were some through carriages between Twickenham and Fenchurch Street, attached/detached at Camden Road. Curves built by the L&SWR at Kew and Barnes to obviate reversing were put into use from 1 February 1862, from which date trains used Kew Gardens rather than Kew and commenced calling at Chiswick and Mortlake. NLR carriages ran from Twickenham on to Kingston from the opening of the line via Hampton Wick on 1 July 1863.

From the opening of Broad Street on 1 November 1865 four of the sixteen weekday trains from Broad Street to Kew Bridge ran on to Kingston. The December 1865 timetable quotes fares from all NLR stations, all HJR stations and Acton to Chiswick, Mortlake, Richmond, Twickenham, Teddington & Bushey Park, Hampton Wick and Kingston.

On 1 January 1869 the L&SWR Richmond Extension line with connections to the N&SWJR at Acton Junction opened and the NLR Broad Street service used the new line. Richmond New became the terminus, through coaches beyond ceased, but the existing through bookings continued. The January 1870 timetable gives additional through fares to Brentford, Isleworth and Hounslow from stations Broad Street to Acton inclusive (i.e. excluding the Bow line and Chalk Farm) changing at Kew Bridge. In October that year fares to these three stations were also quoted from Poplar. The Kew Bridge line gradually lessened in importance, until in 1909 nearly all Broad Street trains ran to Richmond and Kew Bridge was served by a branch train from Acton.

The earliest known through ticket from these services to the L&SWR is the Type FOS1 single shown in Figure 143. The year is illegible but it is unlikely to date from prior to opening of the Richmond Extension line. All other known singles are of Type FOS4 and both NLR and N&SWJR titled tickets are in the down colours of white, red and green. Corresponding returns of Type FOR5 were also in the down colours of yellow/white, blue/red and buff/green. A number of different routing notices were used. Perhaps the commonest was simply "Via Richmond", on tickets from east of Dalston this appears together with "Change at Dalston"; while tickets from Chalk Farm showed "Via Loudoun Road or Camden Town and Richmond". Tickets to Brentford, Isleworth and Hounslow were routed "Via Kew Bridge"; tickets are also known to Feltham, showing "Via Richmond or Kew Bridge" (Figure 144).

Figure 143

Figure 144

Later in the twentieth century through bookings to other L&SWR stations became available, and other routes were used. Possibly the first of these was "via Willesden, Chelsea & Clapham Junction", seen on a single to Wimbledon. After opening of the Metropolitan District Railway's line from West Brompton to Putney Bridge & Hurlingham on 1 March 1880 and the L&SWR's extension from Putney Bridge to Wimbledon on 3 June 1889 (for District trains only, L&SWR ones did not run until 1 July 1889), bookings to Wimbledon and intermediate stations via Earl's Court became available (Figure 145). Tickets for these routes were also in down colours.

In October 1891 return availability to L&SWR stations via

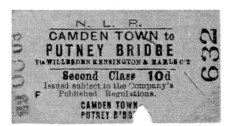

Figure 145

Kensington was day of issue only and from Saturday to Monday, excepting Surbiton and Thames Ditton tickets which were available for four days. Availability via Kew Bridge or Richmond was four days except for stations where the third class single fare was less than 10½d when it was day of issue only and from Saturday to Monday, and except for tickets to Windsor, Ascot, Reading and Wokingham which were available for eight days.

By August 1892 this had been changed so that the four day exception via Kensington applied to Surbiton only; basic four day availability via Richmond or Kew Bridge had been extended to seven days and Thames Ditton was included in the eight days group.

By May 1898 availability was the same by all routes, for distances not exceeding 12 miles or where the third class single fare was less than 1/0½d two days or from Saturday to Monday, except tickets for Brentford, Hampton Wick, Isleworth, Hounslow, Kingston, Norbiton, St Margaret's, Strawberry Hill, Surbiton, Teddington and Twickenham available four days; and tickets for distances above 12 and not exceeding 50 miles available eight days.

From 28 July 1902 Surbiton was omitted from the four day list, which then applied to tickets from NLR stations only. From 30 June 1904 the four day list from NLR stations only was reduced to Brentford and Isleworth, eight day availability applied for distances above 12 and not exceeding 20 miles and for distances above 20 miles six months were allowed.

LONDON BRIGHTON & SOUTH COAST RAILWAY

LB&SCR trains ran from Camden (L&NWR) to New Croydon via Kensington and Crystal Palace from 2 March 1863, and were extended to Euston from 1 May 1863. The service terminated at Crystal Palace from 1 January 1869 and the last such train ran on 30 April 1875. A Kensington - West Croydon service started on 1 June 1863 and a Kensington - New Croydon service on 1 January 1869. There were also Kensington - Brighton and Kensington - Hastings trains in the summer of some years.

LB&SCR stations were also served by L&NWR trains. From 1 January 1869 Broad Street - Victoria trains were operated, replaced from 1 February 1872 by a Willesden - Victoria service that was withdrawn from 1 October 1917. A service between Willesden (Low Level) and Croydon via Crystal Palace commenced 1 May 1875, and was also withdrawn on and from 1 October 1917. These trains initially ran to East Croydon, then to Croydon Central from 1 June 1886 until closure on 1 September 1890 when they reverted to East Croydon.

It is minuted that agreement was reached with the LB&SCR that from 1 May 1863 tickets be issued between NLR stations up to Bow inclusive and stations on the LB&SCR up to New Croydon inclusive, the fares to be computed by adding the LB&SCR local rates from Kensington to the existing NLR fare to Kensington. Return tickets issued on Saturday were to be made available until the following Monday. The tickets were to be of the same colours as adopted by the NLR but with a distinctive stripe, specimen tickets to be prepared for approval (unfortunately none have been seen). Existing tickets via Fenchurch Street to Crystal Palace (by an unspecified route) were to be withdrawn and those via Kensington substituted. There appears to have been some earlier through booking to stations beyond East Croydon, but this was then discontinued with re-booking there becoming compulsory.

The LB&SCR nearly lost their through booking arrangement to Crystal Palace in 1869, due to their late running to Kensington and consequent missed connections.

Figure 146 shows a red second class single of Type FOS4 from Dalston Junction to Wandsworth Common via Willesden and Kensington. Through bookings to the LB&SCR were also available from some stations via Broad Street, passengers finding their own conveyance to London Bridge. A buff third class blank card for such a journey is shown in Figure 147, the back has conditions A2.

Figure 146

Figure 147

Return availability to LB&SCR stations in October 1891 was four days, in August 1892 it was eight days except for tickets from Acton and Kew Bridge to Wandsworth Common and Balham which were available for two days only. In May 1898 tickets via Kensington or via Broad Street and London Bridge were available for two days except for those to Norwood Junction and Croydon which were available for eight days; tickets via Kensington only were available for eight days except for those from Acton to Wandsworth Common, Balham, Streatham Hill and West Norwood which were for two days only. From July 1902 tickets to LB&SCR stations were available for two days or from Saturday to Monday for journeys not exceeding 12 miles, otherwise eight days; from 30 June 1904 eight days applied for all journeys above 12 miles and not exceeding 20 miles, while six months was allowed for journeys for over 20 miles.

LONDON CHATHAM & DOVER RAILWAY

No tickets have been seen but the May 1898 availability table shows the return halves of tickets between NLR (only) and LC&DR stations as being available for 2 days, from July 1902 this was changed to show availability to the South Eastern & Chatham Railway as 2 days for journeys not exceeding 12 miles or from Saturday to Monday, and eight days for

journeys above 12 miles. From June 1904 a limit of 20 miles was placed on the eight day tickets, with tickets for journeys above 20 miles being valid for 6 months.

No clue as to the routing is given, it is assumed to have been via Kensington and the L&SWR trains that ran from there via the West London Extension Railway and Clapham Junction to Ludgate Hill, or via Kensington in L&NWR trains to Herne Hill which operated from 1 June 1880 to 1 November 1890 and again from 1 April 1897 to 1 November 1900. The other possibility would have been travel to Broad Street and then transfer to an LC&DR station.

LONDON TILBURY & SOUTHEND RAILWAY

The first section of the LT&SR was opened to public traffic on 13 April 1854, the line had been promoted jointly by the London & Blackwall and the Eastern Counties Railways and trains (worked by the ECR) were run in two portions, from Fenchurch Street and Bishopsgate, joining at Stratford for the run to Tilbury. The Bishopsgate portions ceased from 1 November 1856, from when all LT&SR trains were Fenchurch Street based, as indeed were all contemporary NLR trains, the two lines diverging at Gas Factory Junction.

Through booking facilities between the NLR and the LT&SR appear to have been provided from opening the latter line. The January 1856 timetable gives fares from stations Hampstead Road to Hackney as follows:

	Single		Return	
	First	Second	First	Second
Barking	1/-	9d	1/8	1/3
Gravesend, Grays, Purfleet or Rainham	1/6	1/-	2/6	1/8
Stanford-le-Hope	2/-	1/6	3/4	2/6
Pitsea	3/-	2/4	5/-	3/9
Benfleet or Leigh	3/6	2/6	5/10	4/2

From March 1856 Southend was added to the table, the fares being the same as those to Leigh. The Gravesend fare included the steamer journey from Tilbury to Town Pier or Rosherville Pier, Terrace Pier being added in October 1856.

In April 1854 passengers changed at Stepney, from NLR trains into the Fenchurch Street portions of LT&SR trains. From 16 October 1854 the NLR provided through Hampstead Road - Stratford Bridge coaches, detached from the main NLR trains at Victoria Park Junction. Passengers to and from the LT&SR then changed at Stratford, very good connections being available. This was not to last, however, LT&SR running via Stratford ceased on 31 March 1858 when all trains were diverted to the new direct line from Barking Junction to Gas Factory Junction. Changing at Stepney was resumed, the ease of connection being further eroded when the through NLR Fenchurch Street trains ceased on 1 August 1866, Stepney then being reached via the shuttle service from Bow. Passengers from west of Dalston Junction also had to change there to reach Bow. This unsatisfactory situation was remedied by the introduction, on 1 September 1866, of a Chalk Farm -Victoria Park-Stratford-Barking through service operated by the NLR, unfortunately abandoned after two months due to congestion at Stratford.

A potentially permanent solution to the problem came with the opening of the curve from Bow (NLR) to Bromley (LT&SR) on 17 May 1869, a daily Chalk Farm - Plaistow service being introduced by the NLR the following day, connecting with most LT&SR services at Plaistow. Through first and second class single and return fares between NLR and LT&SR stations were agreed at a meeting on 3 May. The single fares were:

	Poplar		Bow		Old Ford		Vic Pk		Other NL stations	
	1st	2nd	1st	2nd	1st	2nd	1st	2nd	1st	2nd
Bromley	4d	3d	3d	2d	4d	3d	6d	4d	8d	6d
Plaistow	6d	4d	4d	3d	6d	4d	8d	6d	10d	8d
East Ham	8d	6d	6d	4d	8d	6d	10d	8d	1/-	9d

Any NL station and:		
Barking	1/4	1/-
Purfleet, Rainham, Grays or Tilbury	2/-	1/4
Gravesend	2/4	1/6
Stanford-le-Hope	2/3	1/9
Pitsea	3/2	2/6
Benfleet, Leigh or Southend	3/9	2/9

Return fares were single fare plus one half, rounded down to the nearest penny. Some revision took place from 1 October 1869, and from 1 August 1871 fares between Broad Street and LT&SR stations were made the same as those from Fenchurch Street.

The through service did not pay and was replaced by a Bow-Plaistow shuttle from 1 October 1871, another attempt was made with a through Chalk Farm service from 1 June 1877, but again it was unsuccessful and the shuttle resumed from 1 February 1878. Second class accommodation was removed from the shuttle from 1 April 1893 and the service ceased on and from 1 January 1916. Through tickets were still issued thereafter, passengers walking between Bow (NLR) and Bow Road station on the Whitechapel & Bow Joint line.

In addition to the year-round services summarised here the NLR ran two through trains daily between Hampstead Road and Tilbury via Victoria Park Junction and Forest Gate Junction from 1 July to 30 September 1855, and a through service between Chalk Farm and Barking by the same route in September and October 1866. Through trains on Sundays and Mondays only ran from Chalk Farm to Southend via the Bow-Bromley curve in the summers of 1869 to 1886, calling at all NLR stations and Tilbury. During some years in the same period NLR carriages ran to Thames Haven or to Tilbury in connection with boats to Margate, carriages being attached to/detached from LT&SR trains at Plaistow. There was again some summer through working between Chalk Farm and Southend from 1907 until 1914.

The earliest known through ticket to the LT&SR is shown in Figure 148, it is an Edmondson print on blue card dating from prior to 1 June 1864 when the name of Islington station was changed. The two transverse black lines probably indicated a

Figure 148

Figure 149

destination off the NLR (c/f Figure 3) and distinguished the ticket as second class. Figure 149 shows a yellow single carrying an 1872 date, the audit snip has been cut from the ticket so it is likely that a miniature repeat was printed thereon and that the ticket is of Type FOS1. It is noteworthy that neither of these tickets carry any indication of changing trains; it is therefore tempting to ascribe the first to the summer 1855 Tilbury service (from where the ferry would have been taken to Gravesend) and the second to the summer 1872 Sunday and Monday (which 8 July was) service to Southend.

Other through singles known are in Types FOS3 and FOS4. Tickets from stations west of Dalston Junction carry the notice "Change at Dalston and Bow" (Figure 150), those from east thereof state "Change at Bow" or "Via Bow". Those from Bow, Figure 151, omitted this notice. Tickets to stations beyond Plaistow included that station in their routing notice. As expected, all these are in the up colours of yellow, blue and buff for singles; white/yellow, red/blue and green/buff for returns. As with tickets to GER stations, however, later tickets from Dalston Junction (and presumably any other City Extension station offering through bookings) were in the down colours of white, red and green (Figure 152) for singles, yellow/white, blue/red and buff/green for returns. Tickets from South Bromley, and presumably Poplar, were in down colours, with the notice "Change at Bow".

Figure 150

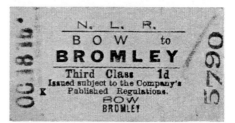

Figure 151

Figure 152

Return availability in October 1891 and August 1892 was, for stations up to and including Barking, day of issue only; for stations Rainham and Dagenham to Leigh inclusive, 2 days and from Saturday to Monday; for Southend and Shoeburyness, 2 days and from Friday to Monday. By May 1898 the second group had changed to stations Rainham and Dagenham to Westcliff-on-Sea (opened 1 July 1895) inclusive, 2 days. From July 1902 return availability was 8 days for longer distances but only 2 days for: all NLR stations with Bromley, Plaistow, Upton Park, East Ham and Barking;

stations Dalston to Poplar inclusive with Dagenham; Old Ford and Bow with Hornchurch; and Homerton to Poplar inclusive with Rainham. From June 1904 return availability was two days for journeys not exceeding 12 miles or from Saturday to Monday, and 8 days for journeys over 12 miles, the table containing a note that all distances were to be taken as over 12 miles except for all NL stations (Chalk Farm, Poplar and Dalston inclusive) with Bromley, Plaistow, Upton Park, East Ham and Barking; Mildmay Park and Dalston with Dagenham; Hackney and Homerton with Dagenham and Rainham; stations Victoria Park to Poplar with Dagenham, Hornchurch and Rainham.

METROPOLITAN DISTRICT RAILWAY

On 1 February 1872 the L&NWR commenced a half-hourly service between Broad Street and Mansion House, known as the Outer Circle service. Beginning on 5 December 1905, one month after District electrification, electric locos were used east of Earl's Court, beyond which L&NWR trains did not run as from 1 January 1909. In March 1912 the Outer Circle service ceased, replaced by a local service between Willesden and Earls Court.

Through NLR tickets to District stations have been seen from stations Dalston Jct to Camden Town inclusive. On tickets to Earl's Court and stations to the east thereof the routing is simply shown as "Via Willesden", except for tickets to Kensington (High St) which show "Via Willesden Kensington & Earl's Court". This last routing is also shown on tickets to stations west and south of Earl's Court, issues have been seen to West Kensington, Hammersmith (M.D). and Walham Green. Tickets are in the expected down colours of white, red and green for singles; yellow/white, blue/red and buff/green for returns. Singles are known in Types FOS1 (Figure 153) and FOS4, returns in Types FOR1 (including that shown in Figure 95 with the H Junc title) and FOR5. It is assumed that as for tickets to the L&NWR the designation "Third Class" was originally used, changing to "Third Class (Parly)" by 1884 and possibly reverting in about March 1900.

One N&SWJR issue is also known, a 1st class single to St James Park on white card, shown in Figure 154, suggesting that (surprisingly) down colours were also used for tickets from the N&SWJR.

Figure 153

Figure 154

A curve from South Acton to Mill Hill Park (Acton Town from 1 March 1910) had been opened by the MDR for freight traffic on 15 May 1899, and from 13 June 1905 this was used by MDR passenger services between South Acton and Hounslow Barracks. One green (down) N&SWJR single of Type FOS4 is known for this service (Figure 155), and one green NLR issue through to Ealing Broadway (Figure 156).

Figure 155

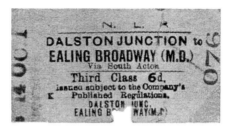

Figure 156

Return availability to MDR stations was day of issue and from Saturday to Monday in Oct 1891, Aug 1892 and May 1898; two days or from Saturday to Monday from July 1902.

MIDLAND RAILWAY

The Midland Railway was one of the lessees of the N&SWJR from 1 January 1871, but showed little interest in passenger services over the line. Reference has already been made to the abortive Moorgate - Richmond service which ran from 1 July 1875 to 31 January 1876. Following this there was a St Pancras - Earl's Court service via the Acton Curve on weekdays from 1 May 1878 to 30 September 1880, and a Cricklewood - Gunnersbury service from 1 January 1894 to 30 September 1902. The only tickets known for any of these services are standard Midland prints from Acton.

TOTTENHAM & HAMPSTEAD JUNCTION RAILWAY

The T&HJR was jointly operated by the Midland Rly and the GER from 1 August 1885, when a GER service between Chingford and Highgate Road commenced. This service was extended to Gospel Oak when that station, with a platform adjoining the HJR station, opened on 4 June 1888. This provided through booking potential from the west, L&NWR titled tickets were issued from HJ Line stations and, more importantly, N&SWJR titled tickets also appeared.

Printed destination tickets (Figures 157 and 158) were in a distinctive style, totally unlike standard NLR tickets, although the style of serial numbers suggests that they were

Figure 157

Figure 158

also Waterlow prints. Singles were in the expected up colours of yellow, blue and buff, returns were white/yellow, red/blue and green/buff. There were also blank cards, printed either "Change at Gospel Oak" or "On Great Eastern Railway via Gospel Oak". Two forms of single are known, one (Figure 159) without a printed indication of where the fare would be entered and therefore earlier, and one (Figure 160) with such indication. Figure 161 shows the outward half of a blank card return, the back is illegible but it is assumed that it will carry conditions B2. Note the "(2.D.)" indication below the routing notice, showing that the return half was available for two days. It is not known whether station numbers appeared on the left hand halves of return tickets.

Figure 159

Figure 160

Figure 161

The T&HJR does not appear separately in the tables of return availability, it is assumed that it was treated in the same way as the GER.

WEST LONDON RAILWAY

The West London Railway, with Kensington the only station, re-opened on 2 June 1862. From that date the L&NWR ran trains from Camden to Kensington in connection with NLR trains from Fenchurch Street to Hampstead Road. From May 1863 the Kensington trains started from Euston; until the opening of Willesden Junction on 1 September 1866 trains reversed at the junction with the WLR, from that date they reversed in the Low Level station at Willesden. A new Kensington and Broad Street train service commenced on 2 September 1867 using the High Level platforms at Willesden Junction. It had already been agreed that all trains would be first and second class only and that fares from Kensington for the new service would be:

	Single		Return	
To:	1st	2nd	1st	2nd
Willesden	6d	4d	9d	6d
Stations Edgware Rd to Broad St	9d	6d	1/3	9d
Stations Hackney to Poplar	1/-	9d	1/6	1/-
Stratford	1/4	1/-	2/-	1/4

L&NWR engines and trains were to work through to and from Broad Street, carrying first and second class passengers by all trains. The division of fares was to be by mileage, with the L&NWR taking one third of the NLR's proportion for working expenses. Willesden and Hampstead traffic to and from Camden Road, Highbury, Dalston, Shoreditch and Broad Street was to be considered as one half carried by each company, with Sunday traffic belonging exclusively to the NLR as the L&NWR ran no trains on Sundays.

The suffix Addison Rd was added to Kensington in 1868, possibly from 1 October when Kensington High Street opened. Uxbridge Road for Shepherds Bush opened on 1 November 1869 and Wormwood Scrubs opened on 1 August 1871, the name being changed to St Quintin Park & Wormwood Scrubbs on 1 August 1892, replaced by a second station of the same name on 1 November 1893.

Services over the WLR became extremely complicated, some of these have been dealt with in earlier sections. This section will be confined to tickets to the three WLR stations themselves.

For many years first and second class tickets to Kensington were distinguished by a longitudinal stripe. From both NLR and N&SWJR stations singles were white with a yellow stripe and red with a white stripe, returns were white/red with a yellow stripe and dark blue/light blue with a yellow stripe. Third class tickets, shown as Third Class (Parly) over probably the same period as for bookings to the L&NWR, from NLR stations were in the (expected) down colours of green for singles and buff/green for returns. The singles are illustrated in Plate 3. No third class tickets from N&SWJR stations are known, it seems likely that colours were as for NLR tickets, a possibility supported by the white N&SWJR ticket of Figure 154.

Singles to Kensington are known in Types LOS1 (Figure 162 -untitled from the HJR), FOS1 and FOS4 (Figure 163), returns are known in Types FOR1 (Figure 164), FOR2 (but with the fare added to the right of the class) and FOR5 (Figure 165). A multiple destination return of Type FOR7 is also known, from Old Ford to Willesden or Kensington (A Rd) or any intermediate station (Figure 166), the half shown is yellow.

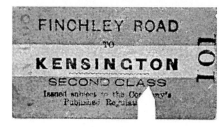

Figure 162

Figure 163

Figure 164

Figure 165

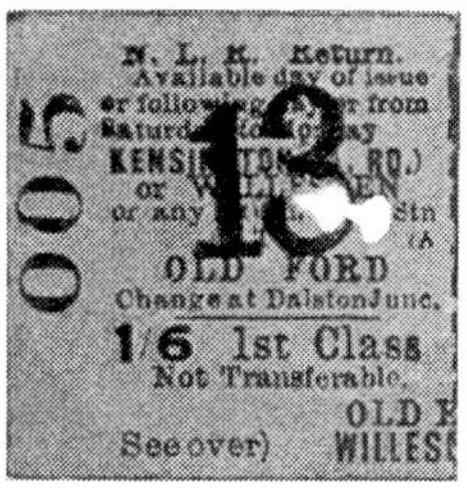

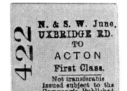

Figure 166

Figure 167

Figure 168

Only first and second class return tickets to Uxbridge Road and to St Quintin Park & Wormwood Scrubbs are known, both NLR and N&SWJR issues are in the down colours of yellow/white and blue/red (Figures 167 and 168).

Return availability was shown as day of issue and from Saturday to Monday in the October 1891, August 1892 and May 1898 tables; two days or from Saturday to Monday from July 1902.

WEST LONDON EXTENSION RAILWAY

It would be inappropriate to detail all the services which worked south from Kensington over the WLER, a very good summary is contained in the Oakwood Press publication *The West London Railway and the W.L.E.R.* by H.V Borley & R.W. Kidner. Suffice it to say that at various times the journey was possible by trains of the GWR, L&NWR, LB&SCR and L&SWR.

Tickets of Types FOS4 (Figure 169, green), FOR2 (Figure 170, buff) and FOR5 (Figures 171, buff and 172, green) to WLER stations are known. The tickets of Figures 171 and 172 are in fact hybrids in that they could also have been used to the District Railway West Brompton station by changing at Earl's

Court. Conditions B1 appear on the back of the ticket of Figure 172. As with tickets to the WLR the designation Third Class (Parly) was probably used over the same period as for bookings to the L&NWR.

Return availabilities were as for the West London Railway.

Figure 169

Figure 170

Figure 171

Figure 172

STEAMERS

It is clear that the NLR had high hopes for the direct train service to Blackwall, the station being located at Brunswick Pier where many of the River Thames steamer services called. On 31 May 1870 specimens of through tickets via the Woolwich Steam Boat Company were agreed for issue from all NLR stations to Greenwich and Woolwich and to all NLR stations from Woolwich, Greenwich and Charlton. The fares were to be the same, as far as practicable, as those between NLR stations and Woolwich via Stratford Bridge, i.e. single 1/- first class and 8d second class, returns 1/6d and 1/-. Of these amounts the railway company took 8d, 5d, 1/- and 7½d respectively. The same principle of fares and division thereof was to be applied for bookings to and from HJR and N&SWJR stations, unless higher fares could be obtained. The NLR supplied ticket cases, dating presses and the tickets themselves, which were required to carry the condition that the boat service was *"weather permitting"*. Unfortunately, none have been seen.

LS&TC Minutes also reveal a through booking arrangement with the River Thames Steam Boat Co during the summer seasons of 1885 and 1886.

BLANK CARDS

Blank cards printed with a specific destination company have been referred to in the sections dealing with those companies.

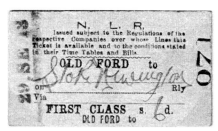

Figure 173

Figure 174

There were other blank cards not so limited, singles as in Figure 173 and returns as in Figure 174. They are known with the NLR title and with the N&SWJR title. Colours were white, red and green for singles and yellow/white, blue/red and buff/green for returns. Conditions B2 appear on the back of returns.

മ⊙ൽ

Chapter Eleven

1912-1923; ORDINARY SINGLES & RETURNS - L&NWR PRINTS

Waterlow's long association with the NLR came to an end in June 1912, at least so far as the printing of edmondsons was concerned. From 1 July 1912 NLR and N&SWJR stations were supplied with tickets printed by the L&NWR at their works in Carlow Street, near Euston. They were in conventional L&NWR formats, varied only by the title of the company. The complex system of colours and station codes was discontinued, all local and foreign ordinary singles and returns being white, red or green according to class.

Figures 175 to 177 show the first types of local single and return. Singles were titled North London Railway or N.& S.W.J.Ry., returns N.L.R. or N.& S.W.J.R. As with the last Waterlow prints, they are known to a single specific destination and to one of a number of alternative destinations, any necessary routing notices following generally those used on Waterlow prints.

Figure 175

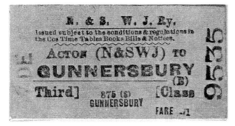

Figure 176

Figure 177

Standard L&NWR practice was to remove an audit snip from the lower edge of the ticket when issuing to a child, the audit snip contained the audit number of the issuing station, the ticket category (e.g. (S) for ordinary single) and the destination. NLR and N&SWJR stations received audit

numbers in the L&NWR series as follows:

14	Broad Street
859	Shoreditch
860	Haggerston
861	?
862	Poplar (East India Road)
863	South Bromley
864	Bow
865	Old Ford
866	Victoria Park
867	Homerton
868	Hackney
869	Dalston Junction
870	Mildmay Park
871	Canonbury
872	Highbury & Islington
?	Maiden Lane
873	Caledonian Road & Barnsbury
874	Camden Town
2	Chalk Farm
875	Acton (N&SWJ)
876	South Acton
877	Hammersmith & Chiswick
878	Kew Bridge
879	Gunnersbury
880	Kew Gardens
881	Richmond (NL)

Note that Broad Street (together with the Hampstead Junction line stations) had been given an L&NWR audit number when these were originally allocated in 1879 and that NLR tickets from Chalk Farm took the existing L&NWR number, again an 1879 allocation. In later years, numbers were allocated in chronological sequence as stations and ticket issuing agencies opened or were brought into the numbering scheme. The main allocation to NLR and N&SWJR stations appears to have been made in late 1885/early 1886. At that time the NLR was still working to Blackwall; if L&NWR titled tickets were issued there as at other Bow line stations then it is likely that it was allocated code 861. Obviously, however, this would not appear on any of the later prints now being dealt with. No relevant tickets have been seen from Maiden Lane, opened on 1 July 1887 and closed on and from 1 January 1917, and no code has been assumed. Chalk Farm was closed on and from the same day, but re-opened on 10 July 1922.

On 1 October 1916 an electric service between Broad Street and Richmond via the HJR began operation, the rolling stock being owned by the L&NWR. Second class accommodation was not provided, and N&SWJR tickets of that class were withdrawn. From 1 January 1917 second class was also withdrawn from the Broad Street - Chalk Farm local service, although it was retained on the Poplar line until 21 September 1925 and on through trains between Broad Street and the GNR until 1 January 1938. Probably from late 1916 second class tickets were also marked "3rd if 2nd is not available", e.g. Figure 177.

The 1914-18 War caused enormous problems for the railways, in common with the rest of the country. A general 50%

increase in fares was imposed by Order in Council from 1 January 1917. This increase, primarily intended to discourage travel, was regarded as a wartime surcharge and tickets generally continued to show the earlier fare. It was not until 1 April 1920 that the new fares were printed on tickets; to avoid confusion, and to remind the booking clerk that a 50% addition was no longer necessary, new tickets were inscribed "Actual Fare"; no local issues have been seen.

"Actual Fare" tickets were short-lived. A further fare increase came into operation on 6 August 1920, ordinary fares being increased by 16²/₃% (to 75% above the pre-war level). Tickets printed after that date used the designation "Revised Fare", as shown in Figure 178. Some time in 1921/22 a decision was taken to abolish distinct foreign prints and thereafter the local formats were used for all printed destination tickets.

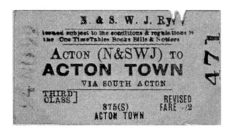

Figure 178

Revised Fare tickets remained current until the grouping on 1 January 1923, when the NLR and the N&SWJR both became part of the London Midland & Scottish Railway, fares being reduced to 50% above the pre-war figures. The grouping did not mean an immediate end to the NLR and N&SWJR titles, some posthumous 1923 prints continuing to perpetuate these. On ordinary singles (e.g. Figure 179 to a foreign destination on the HJ Line) the word "Revised" is omitted, but the class designation is retained wholly at the left hand side of the ticket.

Figure 179

The evolution of local returns was somewhat more involved. It can be assumed that Actual Fare prints (none have been seen) followed the format of contemporary L&NWR tickets and, in common with the first Revised Fare prints, e.g. Figure 180, showed the class at the foot of the return half of the ticket. The class was later reinstated to its position immediately below the half designations, Figure 181, and shortly thereafter those designations were omitted, Figure 182. Posthumous NLR titled tickets showing "Fare" rather

Figure 180

Figure 181

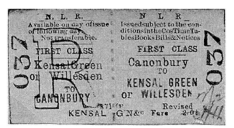

Figure 182

than "Revised Fare" probably appeared in this last format before LM&SR titled prints in the same format appeared.

The automatic machines for 2d third class returns from Dalston Junction continued in use, at least until the fares were increased. L&NWR returns issued from these carried an "AUTO1" or "AUTO2" indication on each half (Figure 183). Continued automatic issue of 1d singles is also likely.

Figure 183

The L&NWR used a different format for tickets for foreign bookings, and NLR and N&SWJR tickets followed suit. The first foreign formats are shown in Figures 184 and 185, singles and returns both had conditions A3 on the back, these were also used on all later foreign tickets.

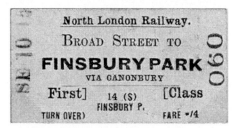

Figure 184

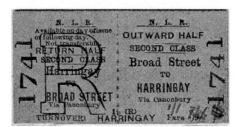

Figure 185

As with local tickets there were then Actual Fare (Figure 186) and Revised Fare (Figure 187) tickets from 1 April and 6 August 1920 respectively, the latter only being printed until abolition of distinct foreign prints in 1921/22. Foreign returns followed the development of local issues in that there were Actual and Revised Fare tickets with the class at the foot of the return half (Figure 188), then Revised Fare tickets with the class below the half designations followed by the omission of those designations.

Figure 186

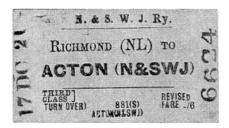

Figure 187

Figure 188

L&NWR returns included the availability as standard on the return half, and this pattern was followed on NLR titled tickets. For most local tickets this was day of issue or following day, this also applied to many foreign tickets. For many through journeys, however, as set out in Chapter Ten, the availability was longer and was shown accordingly. The four day availability for tickets between Richmond or Kew Gardens and Broad Street, initiated on 28 July 1902, also continued (Figure 189).

Figure 189

Blank card singles and returns generally followed the pattern of foreign printed destination tickets, and also carried conditions A3. Figure 190 shows an Actual Fare single and Figures 191 and 192 (the latter with a blank back) illustrate the change from foreign to local format in 1921/22. Note,

however, that on the latter ticket the half designation is omitted from the outward half only.

Figure 190

Figure 191

Figure 192

Local and foreign child tickets (Figures 193 to 195) followed the pattern of corresponding adult issues, the audit snip being cut out before the tickets were supplied to the booking offices. The single of Figure 193 is unusual in showing the N&SWJ's full title, the standard format was initials only.

Figure 193

Figure 194

The Central London Railway opened an extension of its line from Bank to Liverpool Street on 28 July 1912. A booking hall for the new terminus was constructed beneath the forecourt of Broad Street and opened on 10 October, served by escalators from the street. On 23 February 1913 two lifts were installed

Figure 195

Figure 196

to give direct access from the Broad Street concourse and through bookings between NLR and CLR stations were introduced. Single tickets were originally in foreign format, Figure 196, showing "Third Class on NL Ry"; from 1921/22 local format was used with the same class designation. Returns in foreign format are also known, these used the same class designation on the outward half but simply showed "Third Class" on the return half.

Although the vast majority of L&NWR tickets were printed at Carlow Street some issues are found that suggest other printers may occasionally have been used. Only one instance of this is known for NLR titled tickets, as shown in Figure 197. A comparison of this with the standard print of Figure 184 reveals the use of non-standard typefaces; the fare is

Figure 197

particularly worthy of comment as standard prints never showed "d." after the pence!

⊰⊱

Chapter Twelve

REDUCED FARE TICKETS

The NLR and N&SWJR do not appear to have offered the very wide range of reduced fares that was common among the main line companies, possibly because the basic fare structure was quite favourable and/or because of the urban nature of the line during most of its life. The number of existing specimens of reduced fare tickets is relatively low, this Chapter is therefore less comprehensive than those dealing with full fare singles and returns.

EXCURSION TICKETS

Public timetables of 1866 and 1870 do not show any advertised excursion traffic, although excursion trains were certainly run. Thus, the L&STC Minute of 30 April 1867 gives returns of special traffic for the Oxford and Cambridge Boat Race in 1866 and 1867, together with the return for a trip to Crystal Palace on Good Friday in 1866.

The earliest known excursion ticket dates from 1886; Chingford (for Epping Forest) was a popular excursion destination for Victorian London and a number of adult and child tickets to there are known from the turn of the century. The outward half shown in Figure 198 indicates a change at Hackney, using the covered footway opened on 1 December 1885. It follows the ordinary return format of the period, with only the destination being shown in the audit snip, but is printed on card of which the upper half is buff and the lower half green, with a red diagonal stripe. Later tickets showed the fare, and both issuing and destination stations appeared in the audit snip; for these the base colours were those expected on tickets through to the GER, i.e. first class (if any) white/yellow, second class red/blue and third class green/buff if issued west of Hackney and yellow/white, blue/red and buff/green if from east of there, in each case embellished by a diagonal red stripe. A child ticket is shown in Figure 199. There were excursion bookings to some other GER stations via Victoria Park or Bow, again colours were as for ordinary

returns for the same journey, plus the red stripe. Figure 200 shows a buff local half day excursion ticket dating from 1912; there may have been similar first and second class tickets.

Figure 200

Special tickets were printed for excursions on specified dates and for which the number of passengers was guaranteed by the promoter. Waterlow required a premium for printing these, their price from 1 July 1893 being 2/- per thousand. Those known carry dates between 1891 and 1907, the earliest carries the title in full, with the class and "ADULT'S Ticket" at the foot (Figure 201, blue with a white stripe). Later prints had the title in initials on each half, with either "ADULT'S" or "CHILD'S" shown thereafter (Figures 202, yellow/white/ yellow/red/white/red and 203, yellow with a red stripe), in the latter case the audit snip was cut out before the tickets were supplied. The class was either fully spelt out at the foot of

Figure 201

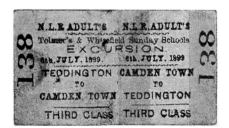

Figure 202

Figure 198

Figure 203

Figure 199

each half as in Figure 202, or shown as e.g. 3rd Class, Figure 203. It appears that there was no standard colour pattern for these prints, so long as they were on multi-coloured card distinct from any of those used for full fare tickets.

Blank cards, e.g. Figure 204, had conditions C1 on the back. They are known in lemon for first class and blue for second class. Figure 205 shows a later blank card printed by the L&NWR, in that company's standard third class excursion colour of buff and with standard L&NWR excursion conditions C2 as used from about 1909 to 1914. L&NWR prints are also known for guaranteed excursions, showing a pre-printed date and the name of the organisation. By the end of March 1915 all excursion bookings had been suspended due to the War, it was not until August 1920 that resumption of such traffic commenced.

Figure 204

Figure 205

CHEAP TICKETS

The heading CHEAP TICKET was used on some excursion returns to the LT&SR, Figure 206 and the non-matching halves of Figure 207, note the "EXC'N" notation as part of the audit snip. The first class outward half is green, the third class is buff with a red return half. Conditions C1 appear on the back. The same heading appears on a half to Maidenhead

Figure 206

Figure 207

on brick red card, shown in Figure 208, without the EXC'N notation in the audit snip but with the same conditions.

Figure 208

Figure 209

Cheap half day tickets were issued from NLR stations to Kew Bridge, Figure 209. Colours were first class yellow/white with a transverse blue stripe on each half, second class blue/red with a transverse yellow stripe on each half and third class buff/green with a transverse red stripe on each half. The backs carried conditions D1. There may well have been similar tickets for other destinations. N&SWJR stations offered bookings in the reverse direction, these are known in two forms as shown in Figures 210 and 211. The former has conditions C1 and is probably earlier, the latter has conditions D1. The outward half is buff, each return half is green and there is a longitudinal red stripe across each ticket.

Figure 210

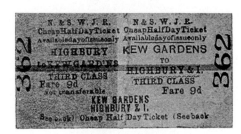

Figure 211

Figure 212

Figure 212 shows the buff return half of a cheap special ticket of 1899, the reason for issue appeared on the outward half, unfortunately missing. However, the back supplies the answer, the conditions indicating that the ticket was only for the use of those employed at the Alexandra Palace and specifying that the owner travels at his or her own risk, and that the Company are under no liability to him or her for loss, damage or injury, however caused.

EXHIBITION TICKETS

Arrangements with the Alexandra Palace had a long history. Through trains to the station there ran from the opening of the Palace on 24 May 1873 and from its re-opening on 3 May 1875, then using an additional bay platform that had been specially provided for use by the NLR. Prior to the re-opening, the Palace Company had requested tickets at half rates for their employees, but this was declined by the NLR as the APCo would not indemnify them against compensation that may have been payable in the event of accident. Clearly, from the ticket of Figure 212, reduced rate tickets were eventually provided, but on the basis that the individual travellers assumed any risk.

At a meeting with the GNR on 12 May 1875 through fares from stations west of Canonbury to Wood Green were agreed as follows, division to be by mileage

	Single			Return			Return plus Admission*		
	1st	2nd	3rd	1st	2nd	3rd	1st	2nd	3rd
Chalk Farm	1/2	10d	6½d	1/9	1/6	1/-	2/10	2/6	1/10
Camden Town	1/-	9d	6d	1/8	1/4	1/-	2/9	2/3	1/10
Barnsbury	1/-	8d	5d	1/8	1/3	9d	2/9	2/2	1/8
Islington	11d	7d	4½d	1/7	1/2	8d	2/8	2/-	1/6

* Admission to Alexandra Palace on 1/- days only; admission on the first Saturday of each month was 2/6d. It is surprising that first class passengers were actually charged 1/1d for admission on a combined ticket!

Basic single and return fares from these stations to Alexandra Palace were 1d higher than the fares to Wood Green, but returns including admission were the same price as for Wood Green. The 1d difference was the maximum allowed by the APCo. It is assumed that fares from stations Canonbury to Broad Street inclusive were settled for commencement of the service. Later through tickets from Bow Line stations are known, with the routing "Via Canonbury. Change at Dalston Junc".

In May 1880 the Palace Company agreed to reduce the proportion of through fares payable to them as admission money by 1d for first and second class passengers and 2d for third class; the fares were reduced accordingly.

First and second class return halves including admission are known from mid-1875, an example of the latter is shown in Figure 213. The first class half is yellow with a transverse blue stripe, the second class is blue with a transverse yellow stripe, colours of the outward halves are not known. Tickets

of 1888 and 1898 are in the format shown in Figure 214. First class colours are not known, second class were blue/red with a yellow transverse stripe on the return half and a lilac Star of David on the outward half, third class were buff/green with a red stripe and blue star. Child tickets were in similar format but with the top line reading "N.L. CHILD'S RETURN", and with the audit snip cut out.

Figure 214

The Alexandra Palace arrangement was not the first to result in tickets including an admission charge. From 1 November 1863 NLR stations from Bow to Camden Road inclusive issued tickets to Crystal Palace including admission on 1/- days at return fares of 3/6d, 2/6d and 2/-. Third class tickets were only issued on days of considerable attractions. These fares represented a loss of 6d on the travel element compared with ordinary fares to Crystal Palace station, which it was agreed would be borne equally by the NLR and the LB&SCR. It is likely that this agreement continued for many years, but no tickets have been seen.

Another popular London exhibition venue in the 1880s was the old exhibition grounds behind the Albert Hall. These were approached from South Kensington station on the MDR, which built a subway between the station and the exhibition grounds. Four annual exhibitions were held, Fisheries in 1883, International Health in 1884, International Inventions in 1885 and Colonial & Indian in 1886, the subway being open only for the last two. In June 1885 Waterlow requested an extra 1d per 1000 for tickets in connection with through bookings to the Inventions Exhibition, which were specially ruled and printed, to which the company agreed.

It is possible that the NLR issued combined travel and admission tickets for all four, but only those for the last one are known, illustrated in Figures 215 and 216 and with conditions D3. First class were yellow/white, second class blue/red and third class buff/green, in each case the three stripes on the return half were red, as was the O indicating

Figure 215

Figure 213

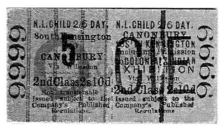

Figure 216

validity only for travel on the Outer track of the circle line. The CIE overprint on the outward half was black, as was the stripe on the outward half that distinguished the 2/6d day tickets.

After 1886 the exhibition scene moved to Earls Court, presenting the American Exhibition in 1887, Italian Exhibition in 1888, Spanish Exhibition in 1889, French Exhibition in 1890, German Exhibition in 1891, International Horticultural Exhibition in 1892, Forestry & Gardening Exhibition in 1893, Industrial Exhibition in 1894, Empire of India Exhibition in 1895 and India & Ceylon Exhibition in 1896.

Tickets specifying the French Exhibition were printed in 1890, Figure 217, note the initials F.E. in the lower left hand corner. Colours appear to have differed from standard, this third class Parly half has a buff upper half and a green lower half. Tickets known from other railway companies suggest that there would also have been NLR prints specifying the particular Exhibition in other years, i.e. with the initials A.E., I.E., S.E., G.E., I.H.E. etc, but by at latest 1897 the generic initials ECE (Earl's Court Exhibition) were used, shown as a black overprint on the outward half and corresponding initials at the foot of the return half, Figure 218. Colours for both adult and child returns were then yellow/white, blue/red and buff/green. Single tickets were also available, in white, red (Figure 219) and green for the three classes; the alternative routes were shown on the back in form D4 for singles and D5 for returns.

Figure 217

Figure 218

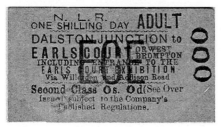

Figure 219

Tickets including admission were also issued for a Royal Military Exhibition at Chelsea in June 1890, the charges being on the basis of fares to Sloane Square plus 9d.

Exhibition halls were also opened at Olympia and through NLR tickets to Addison Road including admission were then issued, as shown in Figures 220 and 221. Colours were white,

Figure 220

Figure 221

red and green for adult and child singles, yellow/white, blue/red and buff/green for adult returns; similar child returns may also have been printed.

Finally for this section, the Royal Agricultural Show was held at Windsor in 1889. The venue for this event changed annually from 1839 until 1902, it was then at Park Royal from 1903 to 1905 before reverting to a different venue each year. For the 1889 Show through tickets including admission were issued from the NLR by the GWR and the L&SWR routes. Only third class specimens have been seen, via GWR adult red with a central green longitudinal stripe and child upper half red, lower half white, each with a black cross on the return half; via L&SWR adult green with a central white longitudinal stripe and child (Figure 222) upper half white lower half blue, each with a red cross on the return half. Conditions D6 appeared on the back.

Figure 222

FORCES TICKETS

Forces on leave were, from 5 December 1890, charged the ordinary third class single fare for the return journey on presentation of an appropriate voucher. Initially, "Soldiers etc." paper tickets were used, but in later years edmondsons were used for some duty issues, Figure 223; the ticket is green

Figure 223

with two transverse red stripes, despite the "Turn over" notice the back is blank. Volunteers were able to obtain cheap tickets on evidence that they were travelling to practice, Figure 224; the non-matching halves are green with a longitudinal red stripe and have conditions B1. A similar print showing "TERRITORIAL" rather than "VOLUNTEER" is also known. In later years L&NWR printed edmondsons were available to forces on leave, Figure 225, this white return half has conditions A3.

Figure 224

Figure 225

SPECIAL AND PARTY TICKETS

The earliest known special ticket is the Edmondson print shown in Figure 14. Figure 226 shows an issue for an unknown event in 1867, the ticket is green with a longitudinal white stripe. Note that this is the earliest known appearance of a titled NLR ticket, but should not be taken as evidence that ordinary singles and returns were titled by that date. Pre-dated tickets for special groups or parties appeared at various times, examples are shown in Figures 227 (white/red with a longitudinal yellow stripe), 228 (red with three longitudinal white stripes) and 229 (green with a white stripe). The ticket of Figure 227 is something of an oddity, it is untitled and what is assumed to be the outward half is on the left, a party

Figure 226

Figure 227

booking to Old Ford must surely have been somewhat unlikely? That of Figure 229 is dated 27 June 1882, a similar half without a pre-printed date is known dated 28 June 1883, on white card with two longitudinal red stripes. It is likely that these were for use by the Bank's volunteer rifle company travelling to Richmond for their annual camp, and that the word "Volunteers" appeared below the remainder of the title on the outward half.

Figure 228

Figure 229

Some organisations were provided with their own bulk supply of tickets, before use each ticket had to be presented to the booking office for date stamping. The ticket of Figure 230 is in the bi-directional green and buff colours appropriate to the journey and has conditions D7, the L&NWR printed non-matching halves of Figure 231 are white with a red longitudinal stripe and have conditions D8. Both arrangements are reported in Officers' Committee Minutes for 18 May 1909. Special third class return tickets between Homerton and Dalston Junction were supplied in quantities of not less than 1000 to the Hackney Union Board of Guardians for use of their employees at a discount of 20% from the ordinary return fare. Special third class tickets available from and to any of the stations Broad Street - Chalk Farm - Poplar were supplied in bulk to the Education Committee of the London County Council for the conveyance of blind school children at 2d for each ticket. In addition, the LCC received a

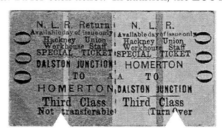

Figure 230

Figure 231

bulk supply of tickets for use between specific NLR stations where the fare was less than 2d, but no indication of cost is given.

Standard Railway Clearing House regulations for pleasure party tickets required that application had to be made at the station at least three days before travelling, and not less than six 1st class or ten 2nd or 3rd class passengers were required. If the application was granted then a form of authority was sent to the organiser for presentation to the booking clerk. The required tickets were then issued at a fare somewhat higher than the single fare to cover the double journey. The non-matching N&SWJR halves shown in Figure 232, on blue card, are the only examples known from the two companies, conditions B2 are on the back.

Figure 232

SPORTS CLUB TICKETS

A circular dated 31 October 1895 announced that special third class return printed card tickets were to be supplied to members of Metropolitan Cricket & Football Clubs travelling to and from their respective grounds on presentation of a proper voucher. The arrangement was to come into operation at once, when the old system of paper vouchers would be discontinued. Examples of the tickets are shown in Figures 233 and 234, the outward half is green, the return half buff and the backs have conditions B1.

Figure 233

Figure 234

WEEK END TICKETS

Cheap week end tickets were issued to some LT&SR stations. Figure 235 shows an outward half, white with a diagonal red stripe, a corresponding third class issue is buff with a similar stripe and both have conditions D2.

Figure 235

PRIVILEGE TICKETS

General Order No 267 stated that on and after 13 October 1890 privilege tickets will be granted to persons in the service of the company and their wives and families at one quarter the ordinary charge to and from stations on the company's system, i.e. stations between Broad Street, Poplar, Chalk Farm, Willesden, Hammersmith and Kew Bridge, but not to Gunnersbury, Kew Gardens or Richmond. Both single and return tickets were available; children under 12 were charged half price with minimum fares of 1d adult and ½d child. Child tickets were to be nipped in the usual way (i.e. the audit snip removed from the lower edge) except when special children privilege tickets were provided, and womens' tickets were to be similarly nipped at the upper edge, those parts to be destroyed rather than sent to audit as with the snips from child tickets.

From 3 December 1890, under General Order No 273, first, second and third class single and return privilege tickets were issued to L&SWR stations on the Richmond Extension line and to selected L&NWR suburban stations; and second and third class returns only to all GNR stations served by NLR trains, and to all LT&SR stations, although to these two companies half fares were available to children under 14. From mid-1892 Bow issued special privilege tickets to Southend and some other LT&SR stations, only available for the annual holiday and only on presentation of special authority; the return availability for these was two weeks.

From 31 October 1894 interchange privilege tickets were introduced, issued in exchange for orders issued by other companies in favour of their employees. These were return only, the outward half available one week and the return half one month. There were reciprocal arrangements with nine other companies, many others being added in later years until the privilege ticket system became almost universal within the United Kingdom.

No Waterlow printed single privilege tickets are known. The earliest known local returns are shown in Figures 236 and 237 (non-matching halves). The availability on the fully printed issue reflects that of contemporary ordinary returns, somewhat surprisingly the blank card does not specify the availability. Standard colours for local returns (and probably also for singles) were white with a yellow stripe, blue with a dark blue stripe and mauve with a red stripe, all the stripes being longitudinal. Conditions E1 appeared on the back.

Figure 236

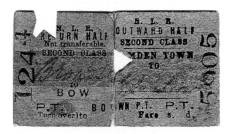

Figure 237

Later printed and blank returns followed the format shown in Figure 238, specifying the outward availability as 7 days and the return as 1 month; colours and conditions remained the same as before. Surprisingly, although tickets from Acton and South Acton (and presumably Hammersmith) were titled N&SWJR, those from Gunnersbury, Kew Gardens and Richmond carried the NLR title.

Figure 238

Figure 239 shows what is probably the earliest form of interchange blank card return. Note that the class is shown as "Third Class (Parly)", by the end of 1901 this had been changed to "Third Class". Unlike local tickets, which showed the name of the issuing station in the audit snip, interchange issues showed the code number of the issuing station, note the small "(1)" in the audit snip of the Figure 239 ticket. Standard colours were red with a white stripe, blue with a white stripe and green with a white stripe, all stripes again being longitudinal. Conditions E2 appeared on the back, these were the same as contemporary L&NWR interchange privilege conditions except for the company initials.

Figure 239

The format for printed destination tickets was similar, as shown in Figure 240; they were the same colours as the blank cards and also carried conditions E2. In addition there was a series of interchange tickets available from any station on the NLR proper (Chalk Farm - Poplar and the City Extension) to any other such station. As seen from Figure 241 these did not have a conventional audit snip, instead the name and code

Figure 240

Figure 241

number of the issuing station were shown prominently at the foot of the return half; no outward half has been seen. Interchange tickets issued at the three Richmond Extension line stations again carried the NLR title.

Tickets printed by the L&NWR from July 1912 followed the formats used by that company and were white, red and green for the three classes. Blank card and printed local singles are shown in Figures 242 and 243, there were similar Revised Fare (and presumably Actual Fare) prints, the second class issues showing the alternative third class if second not available. Initially they carried conditions E3, differing from conditions E2 only in the second line of numbered clause (2). At some time prior to 1920 the conditions were changed to E4, a reference to "Steamers or Boats" having been added in numbered paragraph 2. N&SWJR titled tickets referred to that company rather than the NLR on the back, the later tickets thus having conditions E5.

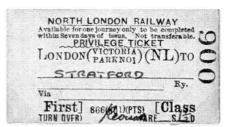

Figure 242

Figure 243

The first L&NWR printed blank card and local return tickets had conditions E6 on the back, whether titled NLR or N&SWJR. Figure 244 shows a fully printed local issue, there were similar blank cards. Later local tickets, including Actual Fare and Revised Fare (Figure 245) prints, carried conditions E4 or E5 according to company.

Figure 244

Figure 245

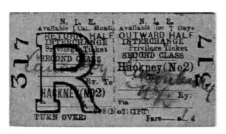

Figure 246

It is thought that interchange singles and returns would initially have carried conditions E3 (or the N&SWJR equivalent), later changing to E4 or E5, an example with conditions E4 is shown in Figure 246.

കൈ

Chapter Thirteen

WORKMENS' TICKETS

LOCAL WATERLOW PRINTS

Draft regulations for the issue of workmens' tickets under the provisions of the Company's Act of last session (30 Vic., cap. 78, Sections 30 & 32) were approved and adopted at a L&SC meeting on 29 October 1867. It is not known when the first workman's train ran, but a notice dated May 1869 appears in the public timetable for January 1870, repeated in that for October 1870.

The notice states that workmen's trains will be run under the Act identified above, tickets being available for one journey only each way per day for one week of six days, at a charge of one shilling. Each passenger was allowed to carry, at his or her sole and exclusive risk, any Trade Tools, not exceeding 28lbs. weight, so packed as not to be inconvenient or dangerous, no other luggage was allowed. The morning departure times were as follows:

Dalston Jct	5.30	6.34	6.49	6.59
Haggerston	5.33	6.36	6.51	7.02
Shoreditch	5.36	6.39	6.54	7.05

Return from Broad Street was allowed by any train after 6.00 p.m., on Saturdays after 2.00 p.m.

In 1869 the 5.30 a.m. train averaged 119 passengers each day during August, falling to 73 in December. In May 1870 it was recommended that this train be extended to Bow, with ordinary fares to be charged between Bow and intermediate stations up to Dalston and the arrangement was approved. In February 1871 an application for a workmens' train from Chalk Farm was declined as limited liability applied only to the City Extension line, this is obviously why there was no fare reduction between Bow and Dalston.

On 7 October 1884 the LS&TC received particulars of the result of the issue of workmens tickets during the eight weeks ending 28 September consequent on extension of the arrangement in pursuance of Board Minute No 3740. That Minute is dated 17 July 1884 and records that it was resolved that the Board of Trade be informed that the Company is willing to extend to their entire system the arrangements now in force for the conveyance of workmen between Broad Street and Dalston. Workmens' tickets to Broad Street were then issued from all NLR stations. On 17 December 1885 the Board approved a recommendation from the General Manager that workmen be allowed to return by any train leaving Broad Street after 4 p.m. instead of 5 p.m. (the change from 6 p.m. to 5 p.m. is not recorded) as at present, as earlier Blackwall and Chalk Farm trains are less crowded.

The earliest workman's tickets covered return travel to Broad Street from Monday to Saturday in a given week. None have been seen from before extension of the system to all stations in 1884, but a rather battered later example is shown in Figure 247. The initials of the days of the week are shown along the top edge, the full wording of the notice at the bottom is "Available for one week from date of issue and only at the Stations named thereon if used for any other Station it will be

Figure 247

forfeited and taken away". Conditions F1 appear on the back. Reading from left to right the stripes of colour are buff/white/buff/green/white/green. The later issue of Figure 248 is in the same colours, the notice at the foot of the ticket has been shortened and is continued on the back, which carries conditions F2.

Figure 248

On 20 October 1892 it was minuted that the attention of the Board had been called to several representations which had been received from time to time for the extension of workman's tickets between all stations, and resolved that arrangements be made for such issue to take effect, if practical, from 1 November. Thus were introduced tickets available to any NLR station as shown in Figure 249. The format was changed to show the initials of the days of the week along both the upper and lower edges, and the conditions were wholly on the back in form F3. Tickets of this type are known from Homerton on yellow, blue and green card, from Dalston Junction on yellow card and from Bow on blue card, each with five transverse black stripes. This suggests a weekly colour change, although if so there is no record of the total number of colours used.

Figure 249

In January 1894 it was reported to the LS&TC that at the suggestion of the Board of Trade and the London County Council daily workman's tickets will be issued on and from 1 March 1894 and that issue of weekly tickets will be

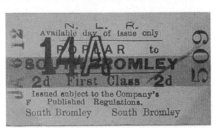

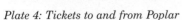

Plate 4: Tickets to and from Poplar

Plate 5: Singles beyond Bow

Plate 6: Workman's Return halves

discontinued from that date. The one shilling weekly ticket was thus replaced by six 2d daily tickets. The earliest known daily issue is shown in Figure 250 and is dated 31 March 1894. Following the example of the last weekly issues the holder could travel to and return from any NLR station. The issuing station is identified by the station code at the foot of the return half, in this case "(11)", i.e. Homerton. Very soon afterwards (a ticket dated 6 June 1894 has been seen) there was a change to show the name of the issuing station on the return half, as shown in Figure 251. Both of these Types have conditions F4.

Figure 250

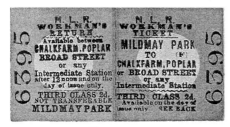

Figure 251

Company practice with these workman's tickets is described in detail in General Order No. 369 dated 27 July 1901. The Order makes it clear that the outward halves of all tickets were orange, and that all bore a letter related to the colour of the return half. The letter and colour were also related to the day of the week on which the ticket was valid, the scheme being as follows:

A	Pink	Thursday
B	Purple	Friday
C	Green	Saturday
D	Red	Monday
E	Blue	Tuesday
F	Yellow	Wednesday

The day of the week to which each letter and colour related was changed periodically, although the order seems to have remained the same. Thus from 28 February 1903, A represented Wednesday; it is known that there were further revisions from 12 March 1906 and from March 1907, and presumably there had been revisions prior to 1901.

Substantial variations occurred in the shade of the colours of the return halves. The pink varied from pale salmon to dark pink, the purple from almost black to a maroon-grey, the green from pale to bright, the red from pale to very dark, the blue from turquoise to grey-blue and the yellow from mustard to brown. One example of each colour of return half is illustrated in Plate 6. All the backs were buff.

The basis of issue is set out in G.O.369 as follows:

"The tickets, which are restricted to artisans, mechanics and daily labourers, are to be issued on personal application at any of the booking offices, and the applicant may be required to give full christian and surname, address and trade, as well as the name and address of employer, and to allow a

reasonable time for ascertaining by enquiry whether the person so applying is an artisan, mechanic or daily labourer.

On persons whose appearance at once denotes them to be *bona fide* workmen, artisans, or labourers presenting themselves and wishing to travel, tickets may be issued without any enquiry being made; but in cases of persons from whose dress, &c., they may appear to be employed as clerks, &c., particulars of their employment should be obtained, and forwarded to me on one of the forms supplied for the purpose.

By the term "daily labourers" it is intended to include warehouse porters and others who receive a weekly wage, but no one employed on an annual salary.

Workmen's tickets are not to be issued to clerks.

These arrangements are also applicable to workwomen as well as men."

Tickets were available at booking offices after 4.00 p.m. for the following day and on Saturdays after 12 noon for use the following Monday.

It is not known when this system of differently coloured daily tickets ceased, the latest issue dates seen are in March 1909. They appear to have been replaced by plain green tickets having the same text layout as the coloured tickets but with no indication of the day on which they were to be used. Some tickets (thought to be later) had a skeleton W on the return half, as illustrated by the non-matching halves of Figure 252, also carrying conditions F4. It seems likely that these green tickets were used until the L&NWR started supplying tickets in 1912.

Figure 252

THROUGH BOOKINGS TO THE L&NWR

On 2 December 1884 it was reported to the LS&TC that on application of the L&NWR workmens' trains have been run from 1 December between Willesden and Broad Street at the following fares: Willesden - Broad Street 6d return; Queen's Park, Kilburn, Loudoun Road - Broad Street 4d return.

This reciprocal arrangement with the L&NWR was later expanded; by April 1906 workmens' tickets were issued each weekday at fares varying from 4d to 5d between NLR stations and Loudoun Road, Kilburn, Queen's Park, Willesden and Kensal Rise, with the following exceptions: (a) Camden Town to Loudoun Road and vice versa; (b) stations Hackney to Poplar inclusive to Willesden; (c) stations between Chalk Farm and Broad Street and Homerton to Poplar inclusive to Kensal Rise; (d) Willesden to Haggerston, Shoreditch and stations Hackney to Poplar inclusive; (e) Queen's Park, Kilburn and Loudoun Road to Haggerston and Shoreditch. Outward journeys were permitted by specified trains no later than 7.22 a.m., with return by any train after 12 noon, excepting expresses. From March 1907 the highest fare had increased to 5½d and the only exceptions were those in groups

(a) and (c) above. At later dates, workmens' bookings became permitted between NLR Main Line stations and HJ Line stations, and between N&SWJR and NLR stations.

Tickets for the through bookings to the L&NWR differed from those for local journeys. The earliest known is the half shown in Figure 253 dated November 1897 and with conditions F5 on the back. By the end of 1900 the format had changed to that shown in Figure 254, with conditions F6. Both tickets are green with white transverse stripes.

Figure 253

Figure 254

L&NWR PRINTS

It is difficult to put forward with any certainty the development of L&NWR printed tickets from July 1912. Both NLR and N&SWJR titled tickets are known, but no record has been found of the date of introduction of workman's tickets on the N&SWJR. It could even have been during the Waterlow era, although no examples have been seen.

The most likely sequence for the tickets of both companies is that plain pale green card was used at first, Figure 255, followed by bright green card with a longitudinal white stripe from mid-1913, Figure 256, and then by white card with three transverse green stripes on each half by mid-1915, Figures 257 to 260. In each case a black skeleton W appeared on the return half. A conditions notice was printed across the full width of the ticket below the title, and standard L&NWR workman's conditions F7 appeared on the back. Below the conditions notice the outward half appears to have been consistently printed with three lines "OUTWARD HALF/WORKMAN/THIRD CLASS". No such consistency applied to the return half, which is known in different versions occupying two or three lines, viz "RETURN HALF/WORKMAN/THIRD CLASS", "WORKMAN/ THIRD CLASS", "(Workman) 3rd Class" and "RETURN HALF/

Figure 255

(Workman 3rd Class)". The variations are unlikely to have any date significance.

Figure 256

Figure 257

Figure 258

Workmens' fares did not increase from pre-War levels until 1 September 1920. A statutory scale then applied to all companies, for journeys up to 2 miles the return fare was 3d, increasing by ½d for each one third of a mile up to 6d for 4 miles and then by ½d for each half mile; an over-riding provision was that no existing fare could be more than doubled. One effect on the NLR was to destroy the simple 2d flat fare structure for any workman's journey on the system, tickets with more limited groups of destinations thus appeared (Figure 259).

Figure 259

A special N&SWJR Munition Worker (Night Return) ticket was available from Kew Bridge to Acton, Figure 260, there may have been similar bookings from other stations.

Figure 260

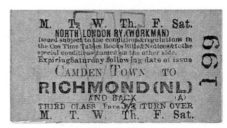

Figure 261

Weekly tickets in L&NWR format were used for some journeys, an example on buff card with a green W overprint being shown in Figure 261; note the small (A) below the destination station. A similar ticket on green card and with (B) below the destination is also known, L&NWR practice was to use the A and B sets during alternate weeks to give a simple check against abuse. Weekly tickets carried conditions F8 on the backs, some could have been printed showing Actual Fare and examples showing Revised Fare are known.

AUTOMATIC MACHINE ISSUES

The September 1894 issue of *The Railway World* includes the following passage at p.334:

" The function of the slot machine has just received a useful extension at the hands of the North London Railway Company. For some time past the weekly workman's ticket has been superseded by a daily issue, so that the passenger missing his train does not lose his 'workman' in addition to paying the ordinary fare. The result of this change was the loss of much time and patience in booking the vast number of morning travellers, notably at Dalston Junction. This delay is now obviated by the introduction of the 'slot' machine, which issues workmen's tickets between Dalston & Poplar, Chalk Farm & Broad Street stations. Should the supply of tickets become exhausted the fare is returned upon pressure of a knob on the machine."

It is difficult to ignore a contemporary report, but no such machine is mentioned in the LS&TC Minutes and no machine issued workman's tickets from Dalston Junction are known. Indeed, ticket issuing machines do not feature in any of the NLR Minutes until the Officers' Meeting of 12 July 1910, when authority was required to purchase three ticket issuing machines from British Automatic Company Limited (BAC) for use at Dalston Junction at £30 each, enabling replacement of a senior booking clerk by a junior, reduction of Sunday labour and easier issue in rush hours. As has been seen in Chapter 5 these machines were used to issue ordinary singles and returns, not workman's tickets.

This Minute reads as though there were no machines at Dalston at that date, assuming that *The Railway World* report was correct there could have been an experimental machine for workman's tickets in 1894. If so, it was probably very short-lived.

BAC were formerly known as Sweetmeats Automatic Delivery Company Limited (SADC). The following report appeared in *The Railway Times* of 7 December 1895, at p.734:

"At the annual meeting of the Sweetmeats Automatic Delivery Company, Limited, the chairman stated that the directors had patented a machine for the automatic dating and sale of railway tickets, and in the short time during which one placed at Homerton Station had been at work over £1,000 worth of tickets had been taken from it. Its operation showed that workmen were willing, indeed anxious, to buy their tickets on the way home from work, if an opportunity was given them for doing so, and this could easily be done by means of such machines as these without throwing any additional work on the ordinary staff; and further, even in the case of those who postponed taking their tickets till just before the train started, the machines prevented all the crowding and confusion that so often took place - in fact, pressure of traffic to any extent could be dealt with by merely placing additional machines at convenient spots. The North London Railway were so pleased with the machine at

Homerton that they had requested further ones to be supplied."

As previously intimated, this machine is not mentioned in the LS&TC Minutes, although the Waterlow contract from 1 July 1896 gives a higher rate of 1/6d per 1000 for printing "*Special Machine Workman's*" tickets. The earliest machine issue date on a workman's ticket from Homerton is 2 August 1895 (consistent with *The Railway Times* report) and it became the busiest station for this class of traffic.

Machines for issuing workman's tickets are known to have been located at Bow, Hackney, Homerton (two machines), Old Ford and Victoria Park, although there is no record as to when any of these came into use. The machines were supplied and owned by SADC under an arrangement whereby the NLR enjoyed free use of the machines and in exchange SADC were allowed to place an equal number of sweetmeat or weighing machines at certain stations without paying rent. Tickets issued from the machines have a skeleton M overprint on the outward half, or M2 if from the second machine at Homerton, and include an A.M. or A.M.2 indication at the foot of the return half, Figures 262 to 264.

Figure 262

Figure 263

Figure 264

They used the same letter and colour system as booking office issues, and also carried conditions F4.

One feature of the machine issues is that some were printed on card significantly thicker than standard. Indeed, it will be recalled from Chapter Three that from 1 July 1899 Waterlow quoted separate prices for special machine workman's tickets and for the same tickets extra thick. However, it is not easy to relate the thicker tickets to particular stations.

The earliest minuted reference to the SADC agreement is in 1910, when the Secretary reported to the Board its expiration on 25 December 1910, it was later agreed to continue for a further 3 years on the same terms as before. From 25 December 1913 the term of the agreement was reduced to one year, continuing thereafter from year to year subject to six months notice.

It was reported to the Officers Meeting on 14 December 1915 that BAC had asked to terminate the agreement due to a large drop in their receipts from the "exchange" machines. They proposed to withdraw these and required the company to purchase or hire the ticket machines. It was recommended that the machines at Bow, Homerton (two) and Hackney be purchased at £25 each and that the machines at Old Ford and

Victoria Park be dispensed with, and this appears to have been acted on.

On 17 March 1921 the Board agreed that the seven automatic ticket issuing machines were not now required and should be taken over by the L&NWR at three-quarters (£142-10-0) their original price. Simple arithmetic confirms that these will have been the three Dalston machines (for ordinary singles and returns) bought in July 1910 and the four machines purchased on termination of the BAC agreement.

It will have been realised from this chronology that machines remained in use during the period of Waterlow printed plain green tickets, Figure 265 and into the period of L&NWR printing. On L&NWR prints an "AUTO" indication appeared somewhere on the ticket, note the lower right hand corner of Figure 266.

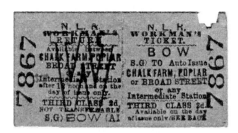

Figure 265

Figure 266

ঙওেঙ

Chapter Fourteen

NON-PASSENGER TICKETS

DOG TICKETS

Dog tickets were issued at NLR stations to "ANY NORTH LONDON STN." at a fare of 3d. They were on white card with an overprinted red square and are known in three types, shown in Figures 267 to 269. For the first two of these the conditions continued on the back in form G1, the third type had conditions wholly on the back in form G2. It is possible that red square N&SWJR titled tickets to any NLR station also existed.

Figure 267

Figure 268

Figure 269

Tickets to destinations on other companies lines carried a red D overprint instead of a square. NLR and N&SWJR titled issues are known in the second and third types identified

Figure 270

Figure 271

above, with either a printed single or multiple destination (Figure 270) or in blank card form (Figure 271).

After July 1912 dog tickets in standard L&NWR format appeared on the lemon card used by that company, both in printed destination (Figure 272) and blank card form and with conditions G3.

Figure 272

ARTICLE TICKETS

It is difficult to be sure of the correct sequence of article tickets. Possibly the first ones used were headed "BICYCLE TRICYCLE, PERAMBULATOR &c", as shown in Figures 273 and 274, each on white card with a transverse red stripe. These are known in printed destination form and in blank card form with pre-printed fares of 6d and 1s or with no fare shown.

Figure 273

Scales of charges and conditions of carriage for articles were set by the Railway Clearing House and adhered to by most companies. From 1 September 1903 orange bicycle tickets were brought into general use, having conditions as to the Company's liability for loss or damage and the NLR and N&SWJR probably followed this practice from that date. Printed destination and blank card tickets are known from

Figure 274

Figure 279

both companies and examples are shown in Figures 275 and 276, conditions H1 are on the back. These conditions refer to the purchase of an extra insurance ticket for one penny; general practice was to print these on blue card and both companies probably followed suit, although no examples have been seen.

Figure 275

Figure 276

Use of separate bicycle tickets may then have led to amendment of the heading of general article tickets to read "TRICYCLE, PERAMBULATOR &c" as shown in Figure 277, again on white card with a red stripe, these being superseded by tickets headed "PERAMBULATOR, MAIL CART &c" (Figure 278). Folding mail carts were charged at lower rates, it is thought that special series of edmondsons for this traffic were introduced in 1912, printed destination tickets with a

Figure 277

Figure 278

red FM overprint are known, as illustrated in Figure 279.

After July 1912 tickets printed by the L&NWR appeared, bicycle tickets on orange card with conditions H1 (Figures 280 and 281), perambulator or child's mail cart tickets on lemon card (Figures 282 and 283) and child's folding mail cart tickets on brown card, initially with conditions H2 and later with blank backs.

Figure 280

Figure 281

Figure 282

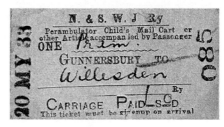

Figure 283

PLATFORM TICKETS

This account of NLR tickets closes with the final type of edmondson to be considered, the platform ticket. The date of introduction of these at NLR stations is not known, but only one format is thought to have been used, printed by the L&NWR as shown in Figure 284. Conditions K1 appear on the back.

In addition to Bow, tickets are known from Broad Street, Canonbury, Dalston Jct, Hackney, Old Ford, Poplar (E.I.Rd.), Victoria Park and Victoria Park (No.2). A London Midland & Scottish Railway (Western Division) booklet entitled *"Instructions to Ticket Inspectors etc"* dated April 1923 includes a full listing of stations then issuing platform tickets. In addition to those given above, edmondsons were said to be

Figure 284

issued at the booking offices at Camden Town, Highbury & Islington and Homerton; there is also an indication of automatic machine tickets issued at Brondesbury. It is likely that these stations also had NLR titled platform tickets.

෨෬

Appendix – Conditions on the backs of NLR tickets

Ordinary Singles and some other Types

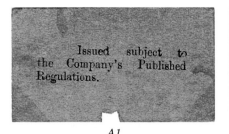

Issued subject to the Company's Published Regulations.

A1

Issued subject to the Regulations of the respective Companies over whose Lines this Ticket is available and to the Conditions stated in their Time Tables, and Bills.

A2

This through Ticket is issued subject to the conditions and regulations referred to in the Time Tables Books Bills and Notices of the respective Cos. and Proprietors on whose Railways Coaches or Steamboats it is available and the holder by accepting it agrees that the respective Cos. and Proprietors are not to be liable for any loss damage injury delay or detention occasioned arising off their respective Railways Coaches or Steamboats. The contract and liability of each Co. and Proprietor are limited to their own Railways Coaches and Steamboats. Not transferable and if used in contravention of the Cos. and Proprietors conditions and regulations it will be forfeited and the full fare charged.

A3

Ordinary Returns and some other Types

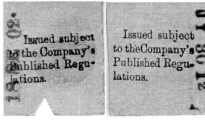

Issued subject to the Company's Published Regulations.

Issued subject to the Company's Published Regulations.

B1

This Ticket is available only on the date stamped hereon, & for one journey only each way. Issued subject to the Companys Published Regulations.

This Ticket is available only on the date stamped hereon, & for one journey only each way. It must be presented whole at the Booking Office to be dated before the journey is commenced otherwise it is not valid. Issued subject to the Companys Published Regulations.

B2

Excursion and other Reduced Fare Tickets

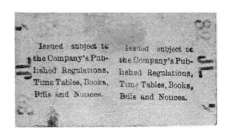

Issued subject to the Company's Published Regulations, Time Tables, Books, Bills and Notices.

Issued subject to the Company's Published Regulations, Time Tables, Books, Bills and Notices.

C1

NOTICE.

Issued subject to the conditions & regulations in the Co's Time Tables & Notices & Excursion & other Bills.

C2

This Ticket is only available to and from the Stations named hereon and the passenger using it on the outward or return journey at any Station short of or beyond that to which it is available, or travelling by any other than the advertised trains will forfeit the Ticket and be charged the ordinary fare.

This Ticket is only available to and from the Stations named hereon and the passenger using it on the outward or return journey at any Station short of or beyond that to which it is available or travelling by any other than the advertised trains will forfeit the Ticket and be charged the ordinary fare.

D1

This through Ticket is issued subject to the conditions and regulations referred to in the Time Tables, Books, Bills and Notices of the respective Companies on whose Railways it is available.

D2

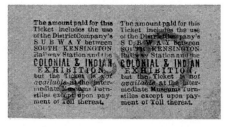

The amount paid for this Ticket includes the use of the District Company's SUBWAY between SOUTH KENSINGTON Railway Station and the COLONIAL & INDIAN EXHIBITION but the Ticket is not available at the intermediate Museum Turnstiles except upon payment of Toll thereat.

The amount paid for this Ticket includes the use of the District Company's SUBWAY between SOUTH KENSINGTON Railway Station and the COLONIAL & INDIAN EXHIBITION but the Ticket is not available at the intermediate Museum Turnstiles except upon payment of Toll thereat.

D3

Excursion and other Reduced Fare Tickets (continued)

This ticket is available at Passengers option either at ...S COURT, WEST ...MPTON (L.&N.W. or DISTRICT) or WEST KENSINGTON Stations

D4

This Ticket is available at Passengers option either from EARLSCOURT WESTBROMPT (L.&N.W. or D...RICT) or WE...FENSINGTON

D5

Issued subject to the Company's Published Regulations, Time Tables, Books, Bills and Notices

D6

This Ticket is available only on the date stamped hereon, & for one journey only each way. Issued subject to the Companys Published Regulations.

This Ticket is available only on the date stamped hereon,& for one journey only each way. It must be presented whole at the Booking Office to be dated before the journey is commenced otherwise it is not valid.

Issued subject to the Companys Published Regulations.

D7

Issued subject to the conditions & regulations in the Co's Time Tables Books Bills & Notices. This Ticket ... Presented at the ... Office to be dated the journey is comm... otherwise it is not y...

14 AU 17

D8

Privilege Tickets

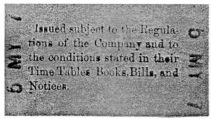

Issued subject to the Regulations of the Company and to the conditions stated in their Time Tables Books, Bills, and Notices.

E1

Privilege Tickets are not transferable, and any person disposing of or making improper use of them will be liable to prosecution & in addition will be dismissed from the service of the Company by whom he is employed. The tickets are issued subject (1) to the general rules and regulations of the Company over whose line the holder is travelling, and (2) to the condition that the N. Ry. Company and all other Companies over whose railways they shall be available, are held free from any responsibility or liability for any loss or injury sustained by persons travelling with them arising from any cause whatever. And the use of the tickets shall be taken as an agreement by the holder to be bound by such rules, regulations, and conditions.

E2

Privilege Tickets are not transferable, and any person disposing of or making improper use of them will be liable to prosecution & in addition will be dismissed from the service of the Company by whom he is employed. The tickets are issued subject (1) to the general rules and regulations of the Company over whose line the holder is travelling, and (2) to the condition that the North London Ry. Co. & all other Companies over whose railways they shall be available, are held free from any responsibility or liability for any loss or injury sustained by persons travelling with them arising from any cause whatever. And the use of the tickets shall be taken as an agreement by the holder to be bound by such rules, regulations and conditions.

E3

Privilege Tickets are not transferable, and any person disposing of or making improper use of them will be liable to prosecution & in addition will be dismissed from the service of the Company by whom he is employed. The tickets are issued subject (1) to the general rules and regulations of the Company over whose line the holder is travelling, and (2) to the condition that the North London Ry. Company & all other Companies over whose railways or by whose Steamers or Boats they shall be available, are held free from any responsibility or liability for any loss or injury sustained by persons travelling with them arising from any cause whatsoever. And the use of the tickets shall be taken as an agreement by the holder ...

E4

Privilege Tickets are not transferable, and any person disposing of or making improper use of them will be liable to prosecution & in addition will be dismissed from the Service of the Company by whom he is employed. The tickets are issued subject (1) to the general rules and regulations of the Company over whose line the holder is travelling, and (2) to the conditions that the N. & S. W. J. Ry Co. and all other Companies over whose railways or by whose Steamers or Boats they shall be available, are held free from any responsibility or liability for any loss or injury sustained by persons travelling with them arising from any cause whatever. And the use of the tickets shall be taken as an agreement by the holder to be bound by such rules, regulations and conditions.

E5

Issued subject to the conditions and regulations in the Co's Time Tables Books Bills and Notices.

Anyone other than the person in whose favour this Privilege ticket is issued making use of it will be liable to the same penalties as a passenger travelling without a ticket.

E6

Workman's Tickets

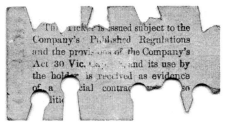

This Ticket is issued subject to the Company's Published Regulations and the provisions of the Company's Act 30 Vic. Cap. ... and its use by the holder is received as evidence of a ... cial contrac ... ...

F1

only a ... Station ... ... used for any other Station ... will be forfeited & taken away. This Ticket is issued subject to the Company's Published Regulations and the provisions of the Company's Act 30. V ... Cap. 78 and its use by the holder is received as ... ... of ... Special contract ...

F2

This Ticket is available for one week of six days from date of issue, and for one journey only in each direction on each day, whilst in force except Sundays, Christmas Day and Good Friday. It is not transferable, and if used by any but the authorised trains the holder will be charged the full ordinary fare from the Starting Station and the Ticket forfeited. The Ticket is issued subject to the Company's Published Regulations and the provisions of the Company's Act, 30 Vic., Cap. 78, and its use by the holder is received as evidence of a Special Contract upon those Conditions.

F3

This Ticket is available for one journey only in each direction. It is not transferable, & if used by any but the authorized trains, the full ordinary fare from the Starting Station must be paid.

The Ticket is issued subject to the Company's Published Regulations and the provisions of the Company's Act, 30 Vic. Cap. 78, and its use by the holder is received as evidence of a Special Contract upon these Conditions.

F4

3 NOV

Available only on the return journey by the trains leaving Willesden as under

Saturdays 12.32 p.m. or any subsequent train.

Other week days 5.17 p.m. or any subsequent train

F5

28 AP. 10

Available on the return journey after 12 noon and on the day of issue only

This Ticket is issued ... ... to the Company's Published Regulations and the provisions of the Company's ... Vic. Cap. 78, and ... use by the holder on the North London Railway is received as evidence of a Special Contract upon those conditions

F6

Available by the authorised Workmen's trains. See Time Tables.

This Ticket is issued at a reduced rate and in consideration thereof is accepted by the passenger on the express condition that the liability of the Company to make compensation for injury or otherwise in respect of the passenger shall be limited to a sum not exceeding ONE HUNDRED POUNDS and that the amount of compensation payable in respect of any such passenger shall subject to such limitation be determined by an arbitrator to be appointed by the Board of Trade and not otherwise.

NOT TRANSFERABLE.

F7

Available for one journey each way daily only, by the authorised Workmen's trains. See Time Tables.

This ticket is issued at a reduced rate and in consideration thereof is accepted by the passenger on the express condition that the liability of the Company to make compensation for injury or otherwise in respect of the passenger shall be limited to a sum not exceeding ONE HUNDRED POUNDS and that the amount of compensation payable in respect of any such passenger shall subject to such limitation be determined by an arbitrator to be appointed by the Board of Trade and not otherwise.

NOT TRANSFERABLE.

F8

Dog and Article Tickets

and subject to the conditions following:-- The Company are not and will not be Common Carriers of Dogs, nor will they receive Dogs for Conveyance except on the terms that they shall not be responsible for any greater amount or damages for the loss thereof or injury thereto beyond the sum of £2,

G1

The Company are not, and will not be, Common Carriers of Dogs, nor will they receive Dogs for conveyance except on the terms that they or any other Company or Companies over whose lines the Dog may pass shall not be responsible for loss, injury, or delay thereto, except upon proof of negligence on the part of their servants nor in any case for any greater amount of damages beyond the sum of £2, unless at the time of booking the Dog be declared of a higher value and a percentage of £1¼ per cent be paid upon the higher value so declared.

G2

The Company are not, and will not be, Common Carriers of Dogs, nor will they receive Dogs for conveyance except on the terms that they or any other Company or Companies over whose lines the Dog may pass shall not be responsible for loss, injury, or delay thereto, except upon proof of negligence on the part of their servants nor in any case for any greater amount of damages beyond the sum of £2, unless at the time of booking the Dog be declared of a higher value and a percentage of £1¼ per cent, be paid upon the higher value so declared.

G3

The Company, and all other Companies over whose lines the bicycle for which this Ticket is issued, is conveyed, will be liable for loss or damage exceeding 10s., but will not be liable for loss or damage up to 10s. unless an extra (insurance) fee of one penny has been paid.

No liability will be admitted unless the loss or damage be pointed out to a Company's Official before removal of the bicycle from the Company's premises.

H1

CONDITIONS.

The Company and all other Companies over whose lines the bicycle, for which this ticket is issued, is conveyed will be liable for loss or damage exceeding 10s., but will not be liable for loss or damage up to 10s. unless an extra (insurance) fee of one penny has been paid.

No liability will be admitted unless the loss or damage be pointed out to a Company's Official before removal of the bicycle from the Company's premises.

H2

CONDITIONS.

The Article in respect of which this ticket is carried is carried at a reduced rate at Passenger's risk and therefore the Co. or Cos. over whose lines it is conveyed undertake no liability for loss or damage or delay to it and the acceptance of the ticket is to be taken as conclusive evidence of an agreement to that effect.

H3

Rail Motor Tickets

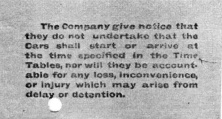

The Company give notice that they do not undertake that the Cars shall start or arrive at the time specified in the Time Tables, nor will they be accountable for any loss, inconvenience, or injury which may arise from delay or detention.

J1

The Company give notice that they do not undertake that the Cars shall start or arrive at the time specified in the Time Tables, nor will they be accountable for any loss, inconvenience, or injury which may arise from delay or detention.

J2

Platform Tickets

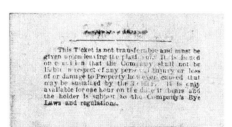

This Ticket is not transferable and must be given upon leaving the platform. It is issued on condition that the Company shall not be liable in respect of any personal injury or loss of or damage to Property however caused that may be sustained by the Holder. It is only available for one hour on the date it bears and the holder is subject to the Company's Bye Laws and regulations.

K1

Backs of Waterlow-printed tickets are:

A1	A2		B1	B2		C1		
D1	D2	D3	D4	D5	D6	D7		
E1	E2		F1	F2	F3	F4	F5	F6
G1	G2		H1					

Backs of L&NWR-printed tickets are:

A3						C2		
D8								
E3	E4	E5	E6		F7	F8		
G3			H2	H3		J1	J2	K1

Other Publications from
The Transport Ticket Society

London Transport Numerical Stage Punch Tickets - Bob Williamson
Checklists of all known "deaf and dumb" type punch tickets from 1933 onwards.

Part 1 - Tram and Trolleybus	£3.50
Part 2 - Central Buses	£3.50
Part 3 - Country Buses and Green Line Coaches	£2.50
Part 4 - Prepaids	£3.50
Part 5 - Miscellaneous	£3.50

London in 1997 - Brian Pask
Comprehensive survey of tickets and ticket systems in the Capital, covering bus, tube, rail and river services. £2.50

INTIS - Brian Boddy
The British Rail Intermediate Ticket Issuing System: a comprehensive guide in two volumes. (*) £8.00

Greater Manchester in 1998/9 - Paul J Smith and Brian Hughes
Complete survey of tickets and ticket systems, covering bus, tram and rail. (*) £4.50

The Tickets of the Grimsby & Immingham Electric Railway - Brian Pask
All known tickets described, with numerous illustrations, faretables and map. (*) £4.75

The Tickets of Hants & Dorset Motor Services 1920-1987 - Andrew Waller
Part 1 - Punch Tickets
Exhaustive history detailing all known punch tickets. Fully-illustrated with tickets, faretables and two maps. (*) £5.50
Part 2 - Machine, Emergency and Office-issued Tickets
Setright, TIM, Willebrew, Almex machine tickets, seasons etc; Fully-illustrated with tickets and one map. (*) £5.50

South Yorkshire Supertram - Fares and Ticketing - 1994-1997 - Dave Aspinwall
A compilation of tables and diagrams, detailing fares, tickets and machine validations. Fully illustrated. (*) £5.50

Tickets of the West Midlands PTE Part 4 - 1983-1986 - Robin Oliver
Details of all known tickets issued in the final years of the PTE as a bus operator. Fully illustrated. £5.00

"Omnibus Tickets" in London - J C Purton, Edited by Brian Pask
The "Omnibus Ticket"-titled issues used in London from horse-bus days onwards. Fully illustrated. £3.50

Tickets of the Liverpool Overhead Railway Company - Trefor David
An overview of the ticket system and tickets of this well-known line which closed in 1956. Fully illustrated. £5.00

Welsh and Scottish Postbus Tickets - Eric C Moles
Checklist of all known tickets 1967 to 1999. Fully illustrated. £3.50

* including illustrations in colour

All prices include postage and packing. Order from the Publication Sales Officer:

Steve Skeavington [X]
6 Breckbank,
Forest Town,
Mansfield,
NG19 0PZ

Why not join The Transport Ticket Society?

For membership details, send two first-class stamps to:

The Transport Ticket Society [X]
4 Gladridge Close
Earley, Reading
RG6 7DL

E-mail: courtney@gladridgecl.demon.co.uk

or visit our website: www.btinternet.com/~transport.ticket